Classroom Walkthroughs to Improve Teaching and Learning

Donald S. Kachur
Judith A. Stout
Claudia L. Edwards

EYE ON EDUCATION
6 DEPOT WAY WEST, SUITE 106
LARCHMONT, NY 10538
(914) 833-0551
(914) 833-0761 fax
www.eyeoneducation.com

A sincere effort has been made to supply the identity of those who have
created specific strategies. Any omissions have been unintentional.

Library of Congress Cataloging-in-Publication Data

Kachur, Donald S.
  Classroom walkthroughs to improve teaching and learning / Donald S.
Kachur, Judith A. Stout, Claudia L. Edwards.
     p. cm.
  ISBN 978-1-59667-133-1
  1. Observation (Educational method) 2. School improvement programs. I.
Stout, Judith A. II. Edwards, Claudia L. III. Title.
  LB1731.6.K33 2010
  371.102--dc22
                            2009040567

  10 9 8 7 6 5 4 3 2

Also available from Eye On Education

Leading School Change:
9 Strategies to Bring *Everybody* On Board
Todd Whitaker

Help Teachers Engage Students:
Action Tools for Administrators
Annette Brinkman, Gary Forlini, and Ellen Williams

The Principalship from A to Z
Ron Williamson and Barbara R. Blackburn

The Instructional Leader's Guide to
Informal Classroom Observations, Second Edition
Sally J. Zepeda

The Principal As Instructional Leader, Second Edition
Sally J. Zepeda

Professional Learning Communities:
An Implementation Guide and Toolkit
Kathleen A. Foord and Jean M. Haar

Professional Development: What Works
Sally J. Zepeda

Motivating & Inspiring Teachers, Second Edition
Todd Whitaker, Beth Whitaker and Dale Lumpa

Get Organized! Time Management for School Leaders
Frank Buck

Creating School Cultures that Embrace Learning:
What Successful Leaders Do
Tony Thacker, John S. Bell and Franklin P. Schargel

From At-Risk to Academic Excellence:
What Successful Leaders Do
Franklin P. Schargel, Tony Thacker and John S. Bell

Dedication

The authors would like to dedicate this book to all educators committed to maintaining an environment of trust, transparency, and truthfulness as they continually strive to make a difference in the lives of their students.

Free Download

The Classroom Walkthrough Models Matrix on pages 145–157 of this book is also available on Eye On Education's web site: www.eyeoneducation.com. Book buyers have been granted permission to print out this Adobe Acrobat© document.

You can access it by visiting Eye On Education's website: www.eyeoneducation.com. Click on FREE Downloads or search or browse our website to find this book and then scroll down for downloading instructions. You'll need your bookbuyer access code: **TWK-7133-1**.

Acknowledgments

In the preparation of this book, we were aware of the many outstanding efforts across the country by educators at all levels exploring, implementing, and assessing the value of classroom walkthroughs as a tool for improving teaching and learning. Walkthroughs are receiving greater attention as principals and other instructional leaders continue to seek strategies aimed at improving instruction with the ultimate result of improved student achievement.

Classroom walkthroughs vary in what they are named, purposes for their use, steps for implementation, length of time for observations, and means for collecting data and providing follow-up from the observations. Common to all of them, however, is that they are brief but focused visits in classrooms that provide data for conversations about teaching and learning. Some models we examined have been around for a number of years and are well known among many educators. Others represent grassroots efforts on the part of educators who designed the tool to best meet their local school or district needs. We do not want to leave any impression that we discovered every possible way this tool is being used to improve schools, teaching, and student learning. The tool is being used in many different ways as illustrated in this book, and new ways are being discovered every day by others. We apologize for leaving out any walkthrough models that are very successful but that we were unable to identify in this publication.

We would like to acknowledge the following educators who generously provided us with invaluable information and assistance and deserve our fullest gratitude for their cooperation in completing this book.

- John Antonetti, Consultant, Colleagues on Call, Phoenix, AZ
- Francis Barnes, Superintendent of Schools, Palisades School District, Palisades, PA
- Laureen Cervone, Associate Director, Northeast Region of the UCLA School Management Program, Los Angeles, CA

- David Cohen, Principal, Midwood High School, Brooklyn, NY
- Joe Crawford, Representative, Learning Keys, Phoenix, AZ
- Carolyn J. Downey, Retired Professor, San Diego University, Palo Verde Associates, La Jolla, CA
- Pam Goldman, Senior Product Developer, Institute for Learning, University of Pittsburgh, PA
- Otto Graf, Jr., Co-Director, Western Pennsylvania Principals Academy, School of Education, University of Pittsburgh, PA
- Pete Hall, Principal, Sheridan Elementary School, Spokane Public Schools, Spokane, WA
- Ted R. Haynie, Director of System Performance, Calvert County Public Schools, Prince Frederick, MD
- Addie Hawkins, Director of Equity, Kansas City, Kansas Public Schools
- Deanne Hillman, Director of Teaching and Learning, Decatur School District #61, Decatur, IL
- Terry Holliday, Superintendent of Schools, Iredell-Statesville Schools, Statesville, NC
- Shirley Hord, Scholar Emerita at the Southwest Educational Development Laboratory (SEDL) and Scholar Laureate for the National Staff Development Council
- Katherine H. Howard, Associate Superintendent, Greenville County Schools, Greenville, SC
- Rhonda Hunt, Principal, Sawgrass Bay Elementary School, Clermont, FL
- Nancy Israel, Executive Director of the Institute for Learning, University of Pittsburgh, PA
- Maryann Marrapodi, Chief Learning Officer, Teachscape, New York, NY
- Moriah Martin, Staff Development Teacher, James Hubert Blake High School, Montgomery County Public Schools, Rockville, MD
- Patricia Martinez-Miller, Director of Faculty, UCLA School Management Program, Los Angeles, CA
- Alexis McGloin, Assistant Superintendent, Penn-Delco School District, Aston, PA
- James G. Merrill, Superintendent of Schools, Virginia Beach City Public Schools, Virginia Beach, VA

- George Miller, Principal, Northern High School, Calvert County Public Schools, Prince Frederick, MD
- Robert Miller, Principal, St. Charles East High School, St. Charles Community Unit School District #303, St. Charles, IL
- Jason Ness, Principal, Niles Central Therapeutic Day School (grades 9-12), Skokie, IL
- Maureen Nichols, Instructional Data Specialist, School District of Philadelphia, PA
- Elizabeth T. Payne, K-12 Coordinator for Health and Physical Education, Fairfax County Public Schools, Falls Church, VA
- Ruby Payne, President of aha! Process, Inc., Houston, TX
- Howard Pitler, Senior Director for Curriculum and Instruction, Mid-continent Research for Education & Learning, Denver, CO
- Douglas Reeves, Founder and Chairman, The Leadership and Learning Center, Englewood, CO
- Martin Semmel, Principal, Bristol Central High School, Bristol School District, Bristol, CT
- Joan Shaughnessy, Program Director, Recreating Secondary Schools, Northwest Regional Educational Laboratory, Portland, OR
- Laura Smith, Principal, Heritage Elementary School, Wentzville R-IV School District, Wentzville, MO
- Dennis Sparks, Emeritus Executive Director of the National Staff Development Council (NSDC), Oxford, OH
- Guy Todnem, Consultant, Project CRISS National Trainer, Batavia, IL
- Deborah Tyler, Principal, Eagle View Elementary School, Fairfax County Public Schools, Fairfax, VA
- Jerry W. Valentine, Professor, Educational Leadership and Policy Analysis and Director of the Middle Level Leadership Center, University of Missouri, Columbia, MO
- Sharon Weber, Principal, Mapleview, Bell Township, and Jenks Hill Schools, Punxsutawney Area School District, Punxsutawney, PA
- Todd Whitaker, Professor of Educational Leadership, Indiana State University, Terre Haute, IN
- Robin Wiltison, Principal, Martin Luther King, Jr. Middle School, Prince George's County Public Schools, Upper Marlboro, MD
- Kathy Witherup, Consultant, Mayerson Academy, Cincinnati, OH

Meet the Authors

Donald S. Kachur is Professor Emeritus of Education from the Department of Curriculum and Instruction in the College of Education at Illinois State University, Normal, Illinois. He subsequently served from 2001-2008 as the full-time Executive Director of the Illinois Association for Supervision and Curriculum Development (Illinois ASCD). Don is a workshop trainer for the Illinois Administrators Academy, the Illinois Principals Association, and the Illinois Association of School Administrators. In the business realm, he served as an executive consultant at State Farm Corporate and participated in the delivery of State Farm Advanced Management Seminars. In addition, Don served as a certified trainer with Motorola, Inc. for their Leadership Development Institutes for school superintendents and Executive Leadership Institutes for school principals. He has published in the NASSP Bulletin (National Association of Secondary School Principals), Phi Delta Kappan, Kappa Delta Pi Record, Journal of Teacher Education, and The Clearing House. He is an active member of the Association for Supervision and Curriculum Development (ASCD), for which he serves on its 18-member board of directors (2007-2010). He is also an active member of the National Staff Development Council, Phi Delta Kappa, and the International Association of Facilitators. He holds his B.S., M.S., and Ed.D. degrees in education from Indiana University, Bloomington, Indiana.

Judith A. Stout is a retired school district administrator and an independent consultant. Judy earned her B.A. from Mercer University, Macon, Georgia and her M.Ed. and Ed.D. from the University of Oklahoma, Norman, Oklahoma. She retired in 2005 with 19 years of educational experience in Lawton Pubic Schools, Lawton, Oklahoma, and nine years in Colorado districts. Her career in Lawton included elementary classroom teacher, teacher of gifted/talented students, staff developer, elementary assistant principal, and elementary principal. After moving to Colorado, Judy was the Director of Elementary Education for Boulder Valley Schools in Boulder, Colorado, for five years and the Director of Leadership in Adams County School District 14, Commerce City, Colorado, for four years before retiring. She has continued to do work in Adams 14 in the areas of preschool supervision and teacher evaluation. Throughout her career, Judy was—and continues to be—passionate about professional development. She was on the team that developed the walkthrough model used in Adams 14. Judy has published in Educational Leadership and the Oklahoma Middle Level Education Journal and has presented at national professional meetings and local district staff development meetings. Her professional association memberships include Phi Delta Kappa, Association for Supervision and Curriculum Development, National Association of Elementary Principals, and numerous local organizations.

Claudia L. Edwards is an independent educational consultant and Graduate Advisor, School of Education and Behavioral Sciences at Cameron University in Lawton, Oklahoma. She earned her B.S. and M.Ed. from Cameron University. She retired in 2002 after twenty-nine years of teaching in the Oklahoma public school system. Her teaching experience ranges from kindergarten through college. As a secondary teacher, Claudia developed a transition program for middle school entry-level students. She also helped create a Saturday program for at-risk students and was the district co-trainer for cooperative learning. During her teaching career, she was an assessor for the National Board for Professional Teaching Standards, served on a variety of school and district-wide committees, supervised entry-year teachers and served as a mentor for student interns. Claudia has presented at numerous state and national conferences. She is also a certified instructor for Structure of Intellect and has co-authored articles for Educational Leadership and Oklahoma Middle Level Education Association Journal. Claudia is a member of Phi Delta Kappa, Association for Supervision and Curriculum Development, and the National Staff Development Council.

Preface

At Heritage Intermediate School in Wentzville, Missouri, Principal Laura Smith and her teachers use Jerry Valentine's Instructional Practices Inventory (IPI) student engagement walkthrough process. Principal Robin Wiltison, Martin Luther King, Jr. Middle School in Prince George's County, Maryland, uses The Learning Walk® routine from the University of Pittsburgh's Institute for Learning. Principal Rey Madrigal, Harlandale High School, San Antonio, Texas, uses the Learning Keys Data Walk model.

Classroom walkthroughs represent an important method for instructional leaders to acquire more frequent profiles of what is taking place in the arenas of teaching, learning, and assessment in their respective schools. They represent another effective tool in a school's arsenal of school improvement efforts. Presently, there are very few books on walkthroughs, and those focus mainly on the implementation of specific walkthrough models. The increasing attention to this tool as a professional development topic is evident by its appearance in an abundance of workshops, articles in magazines, chapters or sections of chapters in books, presentations at conferences, and in recognized programs such as *Accelerated Schools, Project CRISS,* and *Reading First.* In addition, a variety of models, training, and resource materials has been created and marketed on the topic.

Over the past several years, the authors have attended a large number of presentations on classroom walkthroughs at the Association for Supervision and Curriculum Development (ASCD) and National Staff Development Council (NSDC) conferences. The authors, all of whom had their own views and experiences regarding classroom walkthroughs, initially assumed that there would be a high degree of similarity of content in those presentations. To their surprise, the presentations were all found to be quite different in terms of purpose, planning, who is involved, and implementation.

The authors have since found even more variations of how walkthroughs are being designed and used effectively in schools across the country. When examining how different school leaders are using this tool, it has become quite apparent that there is no "one size fits all" model.

Despite the fact that many instructional leaders employ some kind of walkthroughs in order to acquire a perspective of what is taking place in their schools, many are not aware of the varied uses. This book is written to help interested readers acquire that broader sense of classroom walk-throughs and the variety of ways in which walkthroughs can be used as an effective tool for improving teaching and learning.

Woven in greater detail throughout the chapters of this book are eighteen models of classroom walkthroughs sponsored by profit and non-profit companies and organizations as well as grassroots models designed specifically by a single school or school district. This book does not promote any one specific model for conducting classroom walkthroughs but demonstrates the many ways this tool can be used for continuous, systemic, long-range school improvement.

Prior to implementing walkthroughs, school leaders must explore how this school improvement tool can be used and then how the tool can best be designed to meet the needs of their schools. It is also critical for them to think about their school culture and how walkthroughs can be successfully introduced. After this thoughtful planning process, the leadership team will be able to design a protocol to facilitate their school improvement efforts.

The authors examine the following components of walkthroughs:

- purposes for conducting classroom walkthroughs;
- who participates in this process;
- involving teachers in the process;
- focuses and specific look-fors for observations;
- walkthroughs protocols;
- how observable data will be recorded;
- how observation follow-up is provided.

The eighteen walkthrough models cited in detail in this book are:

Models	Source
◆ Bristol Central High School Walk-Through	Bristol Central High School (Bristol School District, Bristol, Connecticut)
Data in a Day (DIAD)	Northwest Regional Educational Laboratory (NWREL), Portland, Oregon
Three-Minute Classroom Walk-Through (CWT) with Reflective Practice	Palo Verde Associates, La Jolla, California
◆ Equity Learning Walk	Kansas City, Kansas Public Schools
◆ Hall Walk-Through	Sheridan Elementary School (Spokane School District, Spokane, Washington)
◆ High School Walkthrough	Northern High School (Calvert County Public Schools, Prince Frederick, Maryland)
Instructional Practices Inventory (IPI) Process	Middle Level Leadership Center, University of Missouri, Columbia, Missouri
◆ Instructional Walkthrough	Eagle View Elementary School (Fairfax County Public Schools, Fairfax, Virginia)
Learning Keys' Data Walks	Learning Keys, Phoenix, Arizona
The Learning Walk® Routine	Institute for Learning, University of Pittsburgh, Pittsburgh, Pennsylvania
Look 2 Learning (L2L) formerly SMART Walks	Colleagues on Call, Phoenix, Arizona
Mayerson Academy Classroom Walk-Through (CWT)	Mayerson Academy, Cincinnati, Ohio
McRel Power Walkthrough®	Mid-continent Research for Education and Learning, Denver, Colorado
◆ Palisades School District Walk-through	Palisades School District, Kintnersville, Pennsylvania
◆ School-Wide Walk-Through	James Hubert Blake High School, Silver Spring, Maryland (Montgomery County Public Schools, Rockville, Maryland)
continued on next page	

Teachscape Classroom Walkthrough (CWT)	Teachscape, San Francisco, California
UCLA School Management Program (SMP) Classroom Walk-Through	UCLA School Management Program (SMP), Los Angeles, California
Walkthrough Observation Tool	Principals Academy of Western Pennsylvania, University of Pittsburgh, Pittsburgh, Pennsylvania

♦ **Grassroots** designed walkthrough models.

We have included research on the value of this tool and have pointed out issues you may encounter as well as recommendations for planning and implementating walkthroughs. It is our hope that in reading this book you will learn:

- the value and practicality of using walkthroughs as a tool in your school setting for improving teaching and learning;
- features from a number of models that can be used in developing your own effective classroom walkthrough process and data gathering practices that meet your school's needs;
- factors within your school setting that need to be considered and addressed in designing and implementing the effective use of walkthroughs.

At the conclusion of each chapter, we have provided some key questions about classroom walkthroughs to reflect on in your role as an instructional leader. We encourage you to think about these questions as you consider how walkthroughs can add value to your school-wide efforts to improve teaching and learning. In the Appendices, we have provided an executive summary of all of the walkthrough models discussed along with contact information, a comparative display of the walkthrough models, and a template for you to design your own school or district walkthrough model.

Contents

Acknowledgments. ix
Meet the Authors. xiii
Preface. xv

1 Introduction to the Classroom Walkthrough as a Tool. 1
   Defining Classroom Walkthroughs. 2
   A Bit of History. 3
   Increasing Interest in Classroom Walkthroughs. 6
   Benefits of Conducting Classroom Walkthroughs. 7
   Instructional Leadership. 9
   Testimonies on Classroom Walkthroughs. 10
   In Summary. 13

2 Research About Classroom Walkthroughs. 15
   Research on Instructional Leadership. 16
   Case Studies and Action Research. 18
   Perceptual Studies. 19
   Research on Professional Learning Communities. 21
   Research on Adult Learning. 23
   In Summary 25

3 Purposes of Classroom Walkthroughs. 27
   School Leaders Citing Purposes of Walkthroughs. 28
   Walkthrough Models and Purposes. 30
   Models Based on Research as a Foundation. 31

Models for Understanding Results of Instructional and Curricular
  Practices... 32
Models That Focus on Student Performance and Opportunities........ 36
In Summary.. 39

4 Involving Teachers in Classroom Walkthroughs................... **41**
Voices from the Field... 42
How Different Models Involve Teachers........................... 44
In Summary.. 50

5 Walkthrough Participants and Training......................... **51**
Who Participates in Walkthroughs................................ 52
Walkthrough Models Requiring Formal Training.................... 54
Walkthrough Models Not Requiring Formal Training............... 60
In Summary.. 62

6 Classroom Walkthrough Protocols.............................. **65**
Guidelines for Walkthroughs..................................... 65
Number of Observers in a Classroom............................. 66
Length and Frequency of Walkthroughs........................... 67
Announced Versus Unannounced Walkthroughs.................... 69
Data Recording and Follow-up.................................... 71
Other Walkthrough Protocols.................................... 72
In Summary.. 74

7 Data Gathered During Classroom Walkthroughs.................. **75**
Moving from a Focus Question to Look-Fors....................... 76
Models Based on Research as a Foundation........................ 77
Models That Focus on Instructional and Curricular Practices........ 79
Models That Focus on Student Performance and Opportunities...... 84
In Summary.. 88

8 Recording Data from Classroom Walkthroughs.................. **91**
Recording Forms... 91
Narrative Forms... 92
Checklist Forms... 98
Combination Forms.. 99
Software Tools for Walkthroughs................................ 106
In Summary.. 110

9 Providing Follow-up on Classroom Walkthroughs............... **113**
Follow-up with Individual Teachers............................. 113
Group Follow-up... 116
In Summary.. 122

10 Additional Factors to Consider about Classroom Walkthroughs. . . 123
   Naming the Process. 123
   Teacher Union Issues 125
   Building Trust for Walkthroughs to Succeed. 127
   The Reluctant Teacher and Walkthroughs. 127
   Managing Time to Conduct Walkthroughs. 129
   Evaluating the Walkthrough Protocol. 130
   Steps in Getting Started. 132
   In Summary. 132
   Final Thoughts. 133

Appendix A: Classroom Walkthrough Model Executive Summaries/
   Contacts. 135
Appendix B: Classroom Walkthrough Models MATRIX. 145
Appendix C: Planning Template: Classroom Walkthroughs in your
   School/District. 157
Appendix D: Learning Walk Newsletter. 159
Appendix E: Walkthrough Feedback Letter. 161
References. 163

1

Introduction to the Classroom Walkthrough as a Tool

The use of the classroom walkthrough does not represent a new educational concept. In many districts, school administrators and other instructional leaders have been conducting such visits as a standard practice for years. However, the nature, purpose, variations of use, and outcomes of the classroom walkthrough as a tool for improving teaching and learning have taken on new meaning. Referred to by such descriptors as *learning walks, instructional walks, focus walks, walk-abouts, data walks, data snaps, learning visits, quick visits, mini-observations, rounds, instructionally focused walkthroughs, administrative walkthroughs, supervisory walkthroughs, collegial walkthroughs, reflective walkthroughs, classroom walkthroughs,* and just *walkthroughs,* the nature of the tool allows for a wide variety of options for its conceptualization and use. The emphasis in this book is on short, informal observations of classroom teachers and students by school administrators, coaches, mentors, peers, and others, followed by feedback, conversation, and/or action. Classroom walkthroughs provide snapshots of instructional decisions and student learning that, over time, create an album of a building's strengths, patterns of practice, and needs.

Classroom walkthroughs alone are not a solution for challenges of school improvement and closing the student achievement gap. However, when instructional leaders choose to equip themselves with a structured, focused walkthrough process and provide individual teachers or the entire school with specific, detailed follow-up, the impact of such instructional leadership will be considerable. As you read this book, think of classroom walkthroughs as a significant instrument in your toolbox of school improvement strategies. Its value will depend on the purpose you seek and the fidelity of its use.

Defining Classroom Walkthroughs

As there are numerous variations of walkthroughs, there are also common features. These features can be identified by examining various definitions of classroom walkthroughs:

Classroom walkthroughs are brief, structured, non-evaluative classroom observations by the principal that are followed by a conversation between the principal and teacher about what was observed.
Center for Comprehensive School Reform
and Improvement (2007, p.1)

The classroom walkthrough is a process of visiting classrooms for short time periods of 5-15 minutes, where the instructional program is observed, feedback is provided to teachers, students talk about what they are doing, and data is gathered to inform curricular decisions.

Walker (2005, p. 1)

Classroom walkthroughs are brief visits to classrooms throughout the school, two to five minutes long, conducted on a frequent basis and are informal and non-evaluative, designed to collect patterns of data that can help members of the professional learning community to continually improve their teaching practices.
ASCD (2007)

Classroom walk-through is used only for short, focused and informal visits to the classroom that are not formal data-gathering situations. Walk-throughs are frequent visits used by the observer to better know the teacher's decision making approach to curricular and instructional decisions.
Downey et al. (2004, pp. 3–5)

The common elements in these statements provide the basic definition of a classroom walkthrough as:

- informal and brief;
- involving the principal and/or other administrators, other instructional leaders, and teachers;
- quick snapshots of classroom activities (particularly instructional and curricular practices);
- NOT intended for formal teacher evaluation purposes;
- focused on "look-fors" that emphasize improvement in teaching and learning;
- an opportunity to give feedback to teachers for reflection on their practice;
- having the improvement of student achievement as its ultimate goal.

A Bit of History

In 1982, Peters and Waterman published a business book that became a best seller. *In Search of Excellence: Lessons from America's Best-Run Companies* shared some of the management techniques of the best-managed companies of that time. Consistent in excellent companies was "intensity of communications." Strong emphasis on such communication in excellent companies was an insistence on informality (p. 287). One particular technique was to have managers leave their offices to walk around and engage with employees through informal exchanges. One company featured in the book was United Airlines with its practice known both as "Visible Management" and "Management by Walking About." Another prominent company was Hewlett-Packard and its trademark management style known as "Management by Wandering Around" (MBWA) (p. 122).

MBWA was basically an unstructured, informal approach to hands-on, direct participation by company managers in the work-related affairs of their workers. This was in contrast to formal and remote forms of management. The overall purpose of these informal visits was for managers to listen to suggestions and complaints of employees, collect qualitative information, and keep a finger on the pulse of the company.

A later book, *A Passion for Excellence: The Leadership Difference* (Peters & Austin, 1985), includes one chapter titled, "MBWA: The Technology of the

Obvious." The authors went into further detail about MBWA, describing it as a means for "being in touch." MBWA promotes innovation and involves listening, facilitating, teaching, and reinforcing values to every member of the organization. The authors further stated, "We will subsequently argue that leading (a school, a small business, or a Fortune 100 company) is primarily *'paying attention'*" (pp. 31–32). In other words, managers of successful companies stayed close to the customers and people doing the work. They were visible and accessible rather than isolated from the daily routines of the business.

The classroom walkthrough is a by-product of MBWA. Among the early pioneers of the MBWA concept in education were Superintendent Tony Alvarado and Deputy Superintendent Elaine Fink when they were at Community School District 2, part of the New York City school system. Under their leadership in the 1980s, walkthroughs became a routine for the district's principals, teachers, and central office leaders. For Alvarado and Fink, their in-depth knowledge of the district's schools and principals came from their own school walkthroughs (Elmore & Burney, 1997).

Alvarado and Fink ultimately viewed principals as the key listeners in the system, and saw being in touch and paying attention as key elements of their leadership. They were strong proponents of principals working closely with teachers as well as providing opportunities for teachers to learn from and coach one another. They then promoted the school walkthrough as the district's primary accountability strategy. Principals observed classroom instruction and environments, arranged professional development opportunities, consulted with teachers and evaluated their classroom practices. As a result, principals captured the concerns and insights of teachers and were able to incorporate their needs and ideas into policy and new strategies. According to Kate Maloy who described the work of Alvarado and Fink in a U.S. Department of Education research report, *Building a Learning Community: The Story of New York City Community School District #2* (1998, p. 17):

> Over the years, the walkthrough strategy has proven to be an effective professional development tool in itself. It focuses principals on their primary task—the improvement of instruction—and encourages them always to be seeking new means of motivating the teachers in their schools, devising opportunities for teachers to develop substantive collegial ties, and deeply informing them about theory, content areas, and best practices.
>
> It also has changed the content of the principals' beginning-of-the-year written plans, which now reflect a much more sophisticated understand-

ing of their schools' and teachers' specific needs in the ongoing struggle for higher achievement among all children.

Subsequently, a number of walkthrough models came upon the scene. The Learning Walk® routine was initially inspired by leadership practices observed in New York City's Community School District #2 as part of the High Performance Learning Communities Project (Fink & Resnick, 2001). In that district, a supervisory walkthrough was used by the superintendent as a high-stakes, on-the-ground review of all elements of a principal's instructional leadership activity. The Institute for Learning at the University of Pittsburgh adapted walkthroughs for use in its partner districts. Participants were focused on improving instruction and learning rather than using the walkthrough as a supervisory or evaluation tool. To mark this new and refined version of the routine, it was renamed The Learning Walk® routine. Further development of The Learning Walk® routine resulted in a set of training tools to ensure fidelity of practice and careful attention to content-specific indicators of teaching and learning in classrooms.

In 1990, Larry Frase and Robert Hetzel published a book, *School Management by Wandering Around.* The book followed current business models and focused on the value of the school leader "wandering" throughout the school and community with a designated purpose and meaning. By wandering around instead of staying behind a desk, the school leader could listen for hints and clues relative to strengths, weaknesses, problems, and solutions. A valuable part of that wandering was frequent classroom walkthroughs and teacher observations. In other words, principals engaged in walking around looking and listening for better ways to do things within the school. Because of the increase in popularity of classroom walkthroughs during the past ten years, the book was republished in 2002.

Another of the early models was Data-in-a-Day (DIAD), which appeared around 1998. DIAD is a walkthrough tool that provides a short but intensive opportunity for a school to gather data about issues that both students and staff view as important. Staff and students collectively observe and summarize data organized around themes they identify in advance and then report to the school leadership for subsequent decisions. DIAD is one of three tools included in the self-study toolkit, *Listening to Student Voices* (2000), developed for K-12 educational leaders and school-based teams interested in including students in continuous school improvement. This toolkit was developed by the School Change Collaborative, a group of regional educational laboratory staff working with K-12 school partners across the country as part of a national Laboratory Network Program.

One educator who has popularized the concept of classroom walkthroughs is Carolyn J. Downey. She, along with co-authors Betty E. Steffy, Fenwick W. English, Larry E. Frase, and William K. Poston, Jr., wrote *The Three-Minute Classroom Walk-Through: Changing School Supervisory Practice One Teacher at a Time* (2004). In her thorough introduction to the philosophy and implementation of this type of classroom supervision, Downey advocates using many informal visits to each classroom to develop a picture of education in the classroom and in the school. She promotes a collaborative approach to classroom supervision, one in which the teacher reflects on instructional and curricular decisions and then plans for improvement; the observer facilitates such reflection on the part of the teacher.

Breaking Through to Effective Teaching: A Walk-Through Protocol Linking Student Learning and Professional Practice (2008), authored by Patricia Martinez-Miller and Laureen Cervone, was the culmination of more than ten years of work. The contributors (teachers, leadership teams, and administrators of schools) were committed to a transformational improvement of student learning. This protocol fills a gap between administrative walkthroughs aimed at teacher or program evaluation and supervision of instruction walkthroughs that focuses on coaching teachers as practitioners. The UCLA SMP Classroom Walk-Through protocol engages teachers in examining student academic behavior. Teachers base walkthrough focus questions on the results of their teaching, allowing change in their practices and improvement in student learning.

Increasing Interest in Classroom Walkthroughs

Let us examine several reasons why walkthroughs are increasingly appearing in the literature and at conferences and workshops for educators.

- **Instructional Leadership:** The principal and other instructional leaders need to further their leadership roles by becoming acquainted with actual building practices. They gather data regarding building needs and strengths that will aid professional development efforts.

- **Professional Learning Communities:** Teachers have traditionally worked in relative isolation. Today, teaching is becoming a public practice with classroom doors being opened to principals, other instructional leaders, and peers. Teachers in professional learning communities are working collaboratively to systematically analyze and share their instructional practices to determine how they can maximize the learning of every student.

- **Data-Driven Decision Making:** The ongoing process of gathering school data helps teachers and schools ask questions about student performance, analyze and organize data to find root causes of performance issues, and implement action plans to improve academic achievement.

- **No Child Left Behind (NCLB) and School Improvement Plans:** NCLB dramatically raised the bar on expectations for all students (including students with disabilities and recent immigrants) to become proficient in reading and mathematics by 2014. This law has increased the level of accountability for schools, causing instructional leaders to assume a more active and visible role in school improvement and the professional development of teachers.

- **Standards-Based Curriculum:** The standards established at the state and district levels must be evident in classroom instruction and student learning experiences.

- **Curriculum and Instructional Initiatives:** Instructional leaders are being called upon to assess the degree of application of newly mandated instructional and/or curricular initiatives in the school building such as Response to Intervention (RTI), reading literacy, formative assessment, and technology integration.

- **Shift from Teacher-Focus to Learner-Focus Supervision:** Rather than watch only teacher behavior, the focus is now to look first at students to see whether they are engaged, motivated, and learning.

- **Increase in Coaching, Peer Coaching, and Mentoring:** Performance data keeps the coach and/or mentor informed on the strengths and needs of the person being coached or mentored.

Benefits of Conducting Classroom Walkthroughs

There are significant benefits for all schools, teachers, students, and observers involved in classroom walkthroughs.

The school gains by:

- collecting additional data on teaching practices and student learning to supplement knowledge about how the school and students are performing;
- increasing school-wide reflection on best practices to increase student achievement;
- acquiring evidence of the impact of curricular initiatives and instructional practices;

- appraising how professional development initiatives are being incorporated into classroom practices;
- identifying professional development needs of the faculty and staff;
- promoting collegial and collaborative conversations that become part of the school culture.

Teachers gain by:

- reflecting on their own instructional and curricular practices related to the school improvement plan;
- engaging in collegial dialogue and reflection about better teaching practices, curricular decisions, and school-wide improvement;
- identifying personal areas of high-need, high-impact professional development;
- receiving individual attention and assistance from instructional leaders.

Students gain by:

- having opportunities to share observations about their learning and suggestions for instructional improvement with educators;
- seeing evidence of and having the opportunity to participate in the entire school improvement effort;
- teaching that more effectively meets their needs and results in improved behavioral and academic performance.

Observers (e.g., principals, assistant principals, mentors, coaches, teacher leaders) gain by:

- maintaining visibility and accessibility that helps build relationships with teachers and students;
- establishing themselves as educational leaders, instructional coaches, or mentors by influencing teaching and learning;
- experiencing a greater awareness of what is taking place in teaching and learning in the school setting;
- determining specific needs in faculty support, mentoring, and/or professional development;
- identifying faculty strengths in specific areas of instruction, curriculum, assessment, and/or classroom management;
- partnering strong faculty members with those in need of support;
- developing better rapport with students.

Instructional Leadership

Current literature reinforces the notion that instructional leadership is a shared responsibility within the school setting (Lambert, 2002; Cotton, 2003; Marzano, 2005; Stronge & Catano, 2008) and the school principal is certainly an integral part of that leadership. It is essential that principals possess tools for engaging staff members in productive conversations about the improvement of teaching and learning. The classroom walkthrough is one of those effective tools.

The classroom walkthrough is a process that assures visibility of principals and provides an opportunity for leaders to see curriculum and instruction in practice. Principals have an opportunity to observe a variety of instructional practices and can engage their staffs in collegial dialogue regarding teacher behavior. As Pete Hall, principal of Sheridan Elementary School in Spokane, Washington, states:

> We contend that the real work of school administrators is not done in the office, at a desk, in front of a computer. Rather, it's done where the action is: where the students are learning and where the teachers are teaching—in the classrooms, in the hallways, and in the supply closets that have been converted into teaching nooks. (Hall & Simeral, 2008, p. 125)

The role of the principal as an instructional and curricular leader is reinforced by the Interstate School Leadership Licensure Consortium Standards for School Leaders (ISLLC). Issued by the Council of Chief State School Officers (CCSSO), these standards serve as the foundation for all that states do to prepare, train, and evaluate school leaders who can get the most from their students and teachers. The ISLLC 2008 standard most relevant to the use of classroom walkthroughs is **Standard 2:**

> *An education leader promotes the success of every student by advocating, nurturing, and sustaining a school culture and instructional program conducive to student learning and staff professional growth.* (ISLLC, 2008, p. 14)

Each ISLLC standard includes a discussion of actions leaders should take to address and reach that standard. Those functions especially supported by walkthroughs and follow-up are:

- to nurture and sustain a culture of collaboration, trust, learning, and high expectations;
- to create a personalized and motivating learning environment for students;

- to supervise instruction;
- to develop the instructional and leadership capacity of staff;
- to promote the use of the most effective and appropriate technologies to support teaching and learning;
- to monitor and evaluate the impact of the instructional program.

The classroom walkthrough allows the principal to (1) be in touch with what is happening in the classrooms throughout the school year; (2) create a collaborative environment where teachers, students, and the principal have opportunities for reflective conversations; (3) pay attention to instruction and curriculum as a participant in school improvement discussions; and (4) exercise the role as instructional leader. The classroom walkthrough represents a valuable data source because it allows the principal an informal way to gather samples of instruction taking place school-wide. Frequent walkthroughs to all classrooms provide an overview of the strengths and limitations of staff so that professional development needs can be planned accordingly.

Principals are important participants in classroom walkthroughs but are only one part of the process. As Linda Lambert professed, "Our mistake has been in looking to the principal alone for instructional leadership, when instructional leadership is everyone's work. We need to develop the leadership capacity of the whole school community" (Lambert, 2002, p. 40). That instructional leadership capacity is expanded as teachers assume a variety of coaching roles such as instructional coaches, peer coaches, cognitive coaches, and literacy coaches. Coaches actively participate in walkthroughs that further enhance the curriculum, improve instruction, change classroom practice, and engage faculty in productive collegial conversations on "best practices."

As you will see in later chapters, many walkthrough models include teachers and in some cases school board members, community members, educators outside of the school or school district, parents, and students. Teachers need follow-up and support, not only from those who supervise them, but also from colleagues, outsiders, and students. They can be inspired by new ideas and new strategies garnered not only from being observed but also being the observing participants in walkthroughs.

Testimonies on Classroom Walkthroughs

Walkthroughs are recommended by staff development experts, university faculty who study K-12 leadership, and school principals across the country.

Shirley Hord, Scholar Emerita at the Southwest Educational Development Laboratory (SEDL) and now serving as Scholar Laureate for the National Staff Development Council, affirms:

> The concept of getting principals into classrooms is a good one and should be encouraged. However, if the walkthroughs become a perfunctory, four- to five-minute visit, with a slip of paper handed to the teacher with no follow-up conversation, we think that sends the wrong message. Without substantive conversations about real classroom practice, not much transfer, reflection, or application to teaching practice will occur. (Hord & Sommers, 2008, p. 104)

Ruby Payne, founder of aha! Process, Inc., and an expert on poverty and mindsets of economic classes, reflects on the value of walkthroughs:

> As a former principal, I did walkthroughs on a daily basis but did not always use a checklist. Checklists are incredibly valuable for all teachers, but particularly for beginning teachers as they help them know what to pay attention to in the classroom. Of particular note for students in poverty is the nature of the relationships in the classroom. The research is clear that if a teacher is perceived by at-risk students as cold and controlling, the student will not learn, even if the teacher's pedagogy is excellent. (R. Payne, personal communication, March 26, 2009)

Doug Reeves, founder and Chairman of The Leadership and Learning Center, sees value in classroom walkthroughs if they are identified by particular characteristics:

> Classroom walkthroughs can be valuable if they: (1) are not judgmental; (2) have the "fingerprints" of local teachers and administrators all over them in terms of design and implementation; (3) provide timely and effective feedback to teachers; (4) are a reciprocal process where the observer and observed learn from one another; and (5) are used primarily for improving teaching and learning in the school. (D. Reeves, personal communication, January 19, 2009)

Mike Schmoker, author of *Results Now* books, speaker, and consultant, says about looking into classrooms:

> Over the years, I have persuaded teachers and administrators into doing something most don't do very often or with a clear focus: tour classrooms. We're not looking for perfection. Nor are we looking for "bad" teachers. We're looking for school-wide patterns with respect to two things: (1) the general quality and substance of instruction; and (2) students' attentiveness—are most of them on task? (Schmoker, 2006, p. 15)

Dennis Sparks, Emeritus Executive Director of the National Staff Development Council (NSDC) shares his opinion:

> When undertaken within cultures of trust and collaboration, classroom walkthroughs conducted by teachers and administrators can stimulate important learning-oriented conversations among teachers and between teachers and school leaders. When combined with other types of evidence, walkthroughs also provide snapshots of current practice that can inform school improvement planning. (D. Sparks, personal communication, March 26, 2009)

Todd Whitaker, professor of Educational Leadership, Indiana State University, Terre Haute, Indiana, and author of *What Great Principals Do Differently: 15 Things That Matter Most*, is quoted as saying:

> In addition to asking individual teachers to observe several of their colleagues while engaged in teaching lessons, we have also found it useful for teachers and administrators to conduct small-group focused classroom walks. In such focused observations, typically a small group (ideally between three and six) of educators visit a teacher's classroom for a group observation. Conducted on a school-wide level, focused classroom walks can be a powerful way to observe firsthand what we are doing in classrooms throughout the building in terms of specific areas of instruction. (Whitaker & Zoul, 2008, pp. 51, 53)

Practitioners in the field using classroom walkthroughs express similar views of the value of this tool. **Rhonda Hunt**, principal, Sawgrass Bay Elementary School in Clermont, Florida, shares the following perspective:

> The CWT process is excellent for answering the question: Is the teacher teaching and are the students learning? It allows for open dialogue with staff and administration as we go down the same path of increasing student achievement. When I walk into a classroom and ask students, "What are you learning?" hearing them restate the teacher's objective for what they are to be learning, seeing all students engaged, taxonomy of learning being used, standards posted and referred to, and the classroom permeates best practice, and I can do this in five minutes, this is truly a win-win for student achievement. (R. Hunt, personal communication, April 10, 2009)

Jason Ness, principal, Niles Central Therapeutic Day School in Skokie, Illinois, explains the value of walkthroughs in this way:

> Working within a specialized population, such as an alternative high school setting for students with significant academic and behavioral

needs, the classroom walkthrough process has served as the primary model in which we have unified our instructional practices and re-conceptualized our behavior management system. Further, the CWT process has allowed for unprecedented collaboration between teachers and administration as well as provided opportunities for younger teachers to observe master teachers at work. In fact, one teacher who is retiring after 33 years reported that his classroom walkthrough was his first opportunity to observe another classroom in all his years of teaching! (J. Ness, personal communication, June 25, 2009).

David Cohen, Principal, Midwood High School in Brooklyn, New York, shares this perspective on walkthroughs:

Midwood's use of walkthroughs has evolved into a critical tool for fostering professional learning. Teachers are learning how to use these walks to gather observed data pertaining to specific instructional tools. The follow-up conversations about instruction and enhancing the learning environment are therefore richer, deeper and far-less theoretical. Simply put, the walkthrough program is changing the culture of professional learning at Midwood High School. (D. Cohen, personal communication, March 26, 2009).

In Summary

The interest in classroom walkthroughs is on the rise because of the benefits derived from the practice. These short, informal observations of classroom teachers precipitate meaningful feedback, reflective discussion, and action. Effectively conducted, walkthroughs will have value for everyone involved as they provide opportunities for all to learn. As you reflect on your role as instructional leader in your school, consider the following:

- How can you use classroom walkthroughs to monitor the implementation of school improvement initiatives?
- What value do you see in classroom walkthroughs for those who do the observing, the teachers being observed, and the students?
- What will be your role in orchestrating the effective use of walkthroughs in your school?
- What are some of the obstacles that will need to be addressed to implement or expand your use of walkthroughs?

In Chapter Two, we review research studies that examine the impact of classroom walkthroughs on instruction and student achievement.

2

Research About Classroom Walkthroughs

It is important to ask the question, "What does research say about class-room walkthroughs?"

The research studies that focus primarily on classroom walkthroughs are limited and have largely been surveys, action research, or case studies determining the value and/or level of use of the process. Thus, a specific answer to the research question is mitigated by the fact that the classroom walkthrough is considered one important tool among many used to achieve school improvement. It is difficult to demonstrate a direct impact between the practice of walkthroughs alone and a school's improvement, although a correlation is indicated in other significant research topics. It would be analogous to trying to determine if a hammer in a toolbox was the direct cause of the construction of a house. Of course, a hammer itself will not result in the total construction of a house because a number of tools are needed to accomplish that outcome. The same is true for classroom walkthroughs. Significant improvements occur when a number of appropriate improvement strategies and tools work in concert with each other within a school culture open to self-examination and self-reflection. For example, peer coaching, mentoring, action research, data-driven decision-making, and group analysis of student work are tools that complement classroom walkthroughs and foster professional development.

Research on Instructional Leadership

Instructional leadership primarily focuses on improving classroom practices of teachers in order to impact student achievement. Numerous research studies, as illustrated below, demonstrate that instructional leadership and teacher effectiveness are the top two school-related factors affecting student achievement.

A systematic meta-analysis of studies intended to examine the effects of leadership on student achievement (Marzano, Waters, & McNulty, 2005) provided data that supported a substantial relationship between leadership and student achievement. Of the 21 specific leadership responsibilities significantly correlated with student achievement, five behaviors particularly related to benefits from walkthroughs are (pp. 42–43, 61):

1. **Communication**—walkthroughs establish strong lines of communication with and among teachers and students;
2. **Intellectual stimulation**—walkthroughs ensure that faculty and staff are aware of the most current theories and practices and make the discussion of these a regular aspect of the school's culture;
3. **Monitoring/evaluating**—walkthroughs help monitor the effectiveness of school practices and their impact on student learning;
4. **Situational awareness**—walkthroughs promote awareness of the details and undercurrents in the running of the school so this information can be used to address current and potential problems;
5. **Visibility**—walkthroughs maintain quality contacts and interactions with teachers and students including making systematic and frequent visits to classrooms; frequent contact with students; and high visibility.

Cotton (2003) published the findings of her narrative review of research literature since 1985 in *Principals and Student Achievement: What the Research Says*. She identified 26 principal behaviors that positively affect student achievement, attitudes, and social behavior. Although most of those behaviors can be somewhat addressed through the use of walkthroughs, the ones most supported (pp. 68, 70) include:

1. **Visibility and accessibility**—effective principals make themselves available to teachers, students, and others in the school community

and frequently visit classrooms to observe and interact with teachers and students;

2. **Collaboration**—effective principals establish an environment in which they and their staffs learn, plan, and work together to improve their schools;

3. **Instructional leadership**—effective principals are actively involved in the curricular and instructional life of their schools;

4. **Classroom observation and feedback to teachers**—effective principals frequently visit classrooms to observe instruction and provide feedback to teachers in the spirit of coaching as well as evaluation.

A synthesis of research on effective principal practice as linked to student achievement was reported in *Qualities of Effective Principals* (Stronge, Richard, & Catano, 2008). The authors arranged those qualities into eight major categories. Although classroom walkthroughs contribute to all categories, the two that have the strongest relationship are "Instructional Leadership" and "The Principal's Role in Student Achievement." Of particular note are the quality indicators or responsibilities and behaviors supported by research under those categories.

"Instructional Leadership" includes (pp. 164–165):

1. **Building and sustaining a school vision** as conveyed by such behaviors as holding high expectations for teachers and students and focusing on school improvement;

2. **Sharing leadership** as exemplified by such behaviors as realizing he or she cannot reach instructional goals alone, believing that staff should collaborate openly, distributing leadership across the school, and creating opportunities for teachers to work together;

3. **Leading a learning community** as demonstrated by such behaviors as serving as a participatory learner with staff and providing staff development that is meaningful to teachers;

4. **Using data to make instructional decisions** as shown by influencing staff to actively analyze data for improving results;

5. **Monitoring curriculum and instruction** as illustrated by such behaviors as possessing knowledge of the curriculum and good instructional practices and spending time in classrooms to effectively monitor and encourage curriculum implementation and high-quality instructional practices.

"The Principal's Role in Student Achievement" includes (pp. 178–179):

1. **The principal's indirect influence on student achievement** as portrayed by such behaviors as working to positively influence instructional practice and ensuring that all students have access to high-quality instruction and to the curriculum;
2. **Focus on school goals and student achievement** as depicted by maintaining a focus on student achievement;
3. **The principal's use of data to guide school success** as delineated by such behaviors as ensuring that student progress data is used to make instructional decisions in the classroom and curricular decisions school-wide and determining whether school goals are being attained.

Crucial to instructional leadership is the principal's involvement in the curriculum, instruction, and assessment efforts across the entire school. It is abundantly clear that principals need tools for engaging teachers in productive and detailed discussions on the improvement of teaching and learning. The classroom walkthrough represents an essential tool for awareness of classroom practices and for building capacity as an effective instructional leader. As part of ongoing instructional leadership responsibilities, school principals must be highly visible through contact and interaction with teachers and students, thus promoting the concept of a learning community.

Case Studies and Action Research

Three case studies of schools and districts that used the *UCLA SMP Classroom Walk-Through* protocol demonstrated positive impacts on teaching and learning. The administrators and teachers at Six to Six Magnet School in Bridgeport, Connecticut, felt that the Walk-Through protocol was a major factor enabling the school to become a results-oriented professional learning community. At Six to Six, all of the educators agreed on a unified vision of what they wanted to achieve and how they would work together to achieve it. At the Antelope Valley Union High School District in Lancaster, California, the Walk-Through protocol enabled the eight district high schools to build professional learning communities that have resulted in improved student achievement. Administrators and teachers at Suva Elementary School in Montebello Unified School District in Montebello, California, expressed the belief that the walkthrough culture contributed to a major growth in student achievement as evidenced by the increase in Academic Performance Index (API) test scores over five years (Martinez-Miller & Cervone, 2008, pp. 55-92).

Lemons and Helsing (2009) cited action research in two school districts that decided to implement learning walks. In one school district, the teachers and administrators expressed satisfaction that the learning walks were successful, though "few can identify tangible improvements in teaching and learning because of learning walks" (p. 479). After two years, the other district's administrators and teachers indicated that they noticed desired school improvement changes and even changes in how the learning walks were conducted. The authors concluded from their research that in too many school districts, strategies such as learning walks are treated as technical solutions that alone "would change teacher practice and improve student learning" (p. 481). Learning walks are too often "treated as a discrete activity, disconnected from other improvement efforts and organizational practices" (p. 483). Where improvements did occur, the district took on an adaptive, systemic, and strategic perspective that altered their values and beliefs as a school district. They learned to work collaboratively in new ways using the learning walk as an important tool among many improvement efforts for leveraging desired changes.

Perceptual Studies

Several studies examined teacher perceptions of walkthroughs. According to Frase's findings (2001), the principal moving in and out of classrooms helps reduce the isolationism of teachers. Furthermore, the increased presence in classrooms provides the principal an improved awareness of both the work of the teacher and factors obstructing optimal teacher performance. Principal walkthroughs result in more highly motivated and highly satisfied teachers. Frase also found that when principals conducted walkthroughs focusing on instruction and curriculum, teachers were more favorable of the teacher appraisal process. Furthermore, teachers held a higher opinion of professional development when principals spent more time in classrooms.

Additional studies have examined the perceptions of school principals about the value of walkthroughs. Dexter (2005) conducted a study to identify principals' perceptions of how the Learning 24/7 Classroom Walk-Through with Reflective Feedback Model (now known as the Teachscape Classroom Walkthrough) provided by the Wyoming State Department of Education could be used to improve teaching and learning. Dexter concluded that principals were positive about the training and believed that the model could make a significant difference in instruction and learning. They also indicated a need for more follow-up training to practice the walkthrough with reflective feedback.

Keruskin's (2005) study examined the perceptions of high school principals who used a Walkthrough Observation Tool from the Principals Academy of Western Pennsylvania and evaluated ways in which the walkthrough model improved student learning and achievement. High school principals and teachers surveyed felt that walkthroughs *did* improve the instruction in the classrooms and ultimately improved student achievement. Results from the study further demonstrated that the walkthrough is a tool to assure that teachers are focusing on the "look-fors," the specific elements of effective instruction or guiding principles of learning collectively identified by the principal and teachers.

An investigation into the effects of supervision on teacher's professional growth was the focus of a research study by Mandell (2006). Principals interviewed for his study expressed the belief that supervision can have an impact on teachers' professional growth, but that the level to which it has impact depends on the type of supervision model used. The majority of principals indicated that the walkthrough model is the most effective method for helping teachers focus on instruction and improve their skills. It allows the principal and teachers to work collaboratively around the instruction and learning taking place in the classroom so that professional growth can occur.

Using the Walkthrough Observation Tool from the Principals Academy of Western Pennsylvania, Rossi (2007) found that from the perspective of the elementary school principals interviewed, classroom walkthroughs positively influenced instructional practices and student achievement. The results demonstrated that teachers shared more frequently with one another and became more conscious of best practices. Principals reported a greater awareness of classroom practice, had meaningful data to share with teachers, and were better-informed instructional leaders.

An examination of the attitudes toward and use of classroom walkthroughs in the state of Illinois was the topic of study by Merrill (2008). Surveying principals and assistant principals from across the state, Merrill found that the majority of the respondents utilized a wide variety of walkthrough approaches. Approximately 75% of the respondents used brief (five minutes or less) walkthroughs. More than half of the principals and assistant principals surveyed reported visiting each classroom in their respective schools at least once every two weeks. A majority of the principals reported that walkthrough data provided curricular insight, improved teacher-administrator relationships, improved instruction, promoted professional growth of teachers, and positively impacted student achievement.

Based on the book *Good to Great* (2001), Gray and Streshly (2008) researched the characteristics and behaviors of principals whose student performance moved from "good to great." Among the behaviors of highly successful principals, as well as those in the comparison group, the researchers found "classroom visits [to be] an important way of ensuring that teachers continued to focus on improving student performance" (p. 110).

Only a couple of studies have demonstrated less favorable teacher perceptions. David (2007–2008, p. 81) reported a study completed by the RAND Corporation in which administrators of three urban school districts found walkthroughs more useful and learned more during the process than did the teachers being observed. Valli and Buese (2007) reported from their study that a district-imposed policy of walkthroughs with a team of observers coming into classrooms resulted in raised teacher anxiety levels. Despite efforts by some principals to alleviate the anxiety, teachers still felt "under the gun" to meet school district expectations (p. 544).

Research on Professional Learning Communities

According to Hallinger (2007), much of the emphasis in the 1980s was on *instructional leadership* that emanated from all of the effective schools research. To be considered effective as an instructional leader, the principal had to have knowledge of effective practices in curriculum, instruction, and assessment and to know how to work with classroom teachers on regular issues in these areas. The focus was on the expertise of the principal as the sole leader for the building. The 1990s witnessed a movement toward *transformational leadership* more focused on capacity building than on leading, directing, coordinating, and controlling others. The emphasis was more on understanding individual needs and empowering individuals. The early 2000s are more characterized by *shared instructional leadership*. The principal is no longer considered the only expert providing all leadership functions.

Although the role of the principal is that of an important participant in a professional community of learners and leaders, professional learning communities are characterized by *shared* leadership and *shared* teaching practices including classroom walkthroughs and other classroom observations. The ultimate goal is, of course, that all feedback becomes part of a larger, school-wide conversation resulting in increased student academic gains. By referring to itself as a professional learning community, a school is signifying its priority not just in discrete acts of teacher sharing. Rather, it is establishing a school-wide culture of collaboration and accountability directed at the critical examination and sharing of teaching and learning practices to improve student achievement.

Hord's research (Hord & Sommers, 2008, p. 9) has demonstrated that professional learning communities (PLC) are comprised of five components (see Figure 2.1).

Figure 2.1
Hord's Five Components of Professional Learning Communities

1. Shared Beliefs, Values, and Vision	Working under a shared vision or common goals, the staff consistently focuses on student learning, strengthened by the staff's own continuous learning.
2. Shared and Supportive Leadership	Administrators and faculty hold shared power and authority for making decisions and work together collaboratively.
3. Collective Learning and Its Application	What the community determines to learn and how they will learn it in order to address student learning needs is the bottom line.
4. Supportive Conditions	*Structural factors* provide physical requirements: time, place to meet for community work, resources and policies to support collaboration. *Relational factors* support the community's human and interpersonal development, openness, honesty, and focus on attitudes of respect and caring among members.
5. Shared Personal Practice	Community members give and receive feedback that supports individual improvement and that of the organization.

While the classroom walkthrough supports all five components, the fifth component, Shared Personal Practices, is most pertinent. Direct and frequent walkthroughs used for gathering information on how well the school is functioning as a professional learning community deepen a PLC's collective understanding of curriculum, instruction, and assessment. Walkthroughs help move beyond identifying and fixing problems to identifying and enhancing student mastery of knowledge and skills. They promote interactive engagement whereby teachers observe and share feedback with other teachers for particular purposes. They enable administrators and teachers to learn from one another about the practice of teaching. Hord comments on the value of walkthroughs in the PLC by saying, "The walkthrough can be tailored for observing teachers as they work as a community and as they implement their community learning in their classrooms" (Hord & Sommers, 2008, p. 136).

Research on Adult Learning

To enhance teacher growth, it is essential to draw from the research literature on adult learning. In the early 1970s, Knowles (Knowles, Holton, & Swanson, 1998, pp. 62–63) identified six crucial assumptions about the characteristics of adult learners. Under each assumption we have added our interpretation of the way they relate to walkthroughs:

1. **The need to know:** The reflective conversations following classroom walkthroughs enable teachers to discover for themselves the gaps between where they are now and where they want to be in becoming better teachers.

2. **The learner's self-concept:** Teachers want to be seen and treated as capable and self-directed. They want to establish their own goals for learning and decide how best to achieve those goals. Walkthroughs enable teachers to have input to their own needs for professional growth.

3. **The role of the learners' experiences:** Teachers have a wide variety of experiences that represent a valuable resource of expertise, and should be the basis for walkthrough follow-up conversations.

4. **Readiness to learn:** Connecting learning opportunities from walkthrough observations to real-life instructional situations promotes teachers' interest.

5. **Orientation to learning:** Walkthroughs provide immediate, relevant opportunities for teachers to learn to perform tasks and deal with everyday problems.

6. **Motivation:** Although teachers are responsive to some external motivators (e.g., better job, higher salaries), the most potent motivators are internal (e.g., student success, desire for increased job satisfaction, job esteem). The feedback from walkthroughs can be a powerful internal motivating factor for teachers.

Lawler (1991, pp. 34–43) identified six keys for facilitating adult learning. The six keys to adult learning are listed below with our summary points and reflective questions related to walkthroughs.

1. **Understand and reduce anxiety:** Teachers may feel anxious and insecure about someone entering their classrooms, or they may be asked to start something new and may be nervous about their own skills and/or

abilities to succeed under observation. With regard to walkthroughs, instructional leaders need to ask themselves:

- Have we been clear in communicating and assuring that teachers know the purpose(s) of the walkthrough?
- Have we been clear in communicating what is expected of teachers and how they are to respond?
- What do we look for in determining how teachers might feel about walkthroughs and what anxieties might exist among them?
- How can we defuse that anxiety and help teachers have realistic expectations from walkthroughs?

2. **Elicit and incorporate expectations**: Despite the goals of the walkthroughs, it must be understood that teachers also have their own needs and expectations. In designing walkthroughs, instructional leaders need to ask themselves:

- Have we considered problems and challenges that teachers would like to address as a benefit of walkthroughs?
- How can we best use walkthroughs to match the needs of teachers with the needs of the school?

3. **Acknowledge and utilize experience:** Teachers bring experiences, knowledge, skills, interests, and competencies as rich resources to the learning process. In fact, both the instructional leaders and the teachers visited in the walkthroughs bring expertise and knowledge to potential learning opportunities. In considering experiences, instructional leaders need to ask themselves:

- How do we learn more about the backgrounds and experiences of all teachers?
- How do we plan for the walkthrough to become an engaging interactive relationship with teachers that allows for the sharing of those experiences to generate new ideas?

4. **Provide and encourage active participation:** Teachers learn more effectively and efficiently when they have opportunities to actively participate in an educational activity. Therefore, walkthroughs need to be planned and designed with numerous opportunities for teacher involvement. In designing walkthroughs, instructional leaders need to ask themselves:

- How will we actively involve teachers in the design, implementation, and evaluation of the walkthrough program?
- How might teachers participate as observers in the walkthroughs?
- What strategies for feedback would teachers recommend?

5. **Identify and incorporate relevant content**: Teachers are usually motivated by a pragmatic desire to immediately use or apply their knowledge and skill. In assuring relevancy, instructional leaders need to ask themselves:

  - How can we make the feedback from walkthroughs meaningful to teachers?
  - How can we help teachers with the immediate application of new knowledge and skills to their classroom?

6. **Facilitate change and growth**: If we hope to promote and facilitate growth and development among teachers in their classrooms, we need to first respect them as learners and professionals and understand their identified needs. In facilitating change and growth, instructional leaders need to ask themselves:

  - How do we demonstrate respect for teachers as professionals and learners?
  - What actions do we take to create a climate where teachers feel comfortable taking risks, sharing, and learning?
  - How do we build on teachers' confidence and engage them in conversations about how their knowledge and skills can be most effectively applied?

In Summary

Specific research on classroom walkthroughs is limited in terms of demonstrating a direct cause-and-effect relationship between the tool and school, teacher, and student improvement. The research that is available largely consists of surveys, case studies, and action research examining perceptions of both teachers and principals. There is a positive correlation using walkthroughs in combination with other research-based practices.

The research literature on instructional leadership and professional learning communities is especially important. Numerous mega-analyses of research studies on instructional leadership indicate the walkthrough as a tool for increasing the principal's awareness of classroom practice and planning for professional development, thereby impacting student achievement.

Other research studies promote the value of walkthroughs as a contributing factor to the creation of professional learning communities, resulting in increased student academic achievement. Walkthroughs afford opportunities for collaboration, sharing of personal practices, and increased understanding of the curriculum, instruction, and assessment as found in professional learning communities.

Finally, research was reviewed on adult learning because the walkthrough is a tool for the observers and observed to learn together. Effective teachers want constructive feedback on their practice, and what could be more important than principals, peers, and other observers providing feedback through a collaborative conversation?

As you reflect on your role as instructional leader in your school, consider the following:

- What is your vision of walkthroughs as a tool for your own instructional leadership?
- What features of your school culture need to be in place for walkthroughs to be accepted and valued?
- How will you incorporate the research on adult learning in how you will conduct walkthroughs?

Chapter Three will help you begin thinking about purposes for using walkthroughs as a tool to improve teaching and learning and introduce some of the many well-defined models and purposes.

3

Purposes of Classroom Walkthroughs

In the first chapter, we presented information on why there is increasing interest in classroom walkthroughs and the benefits of these walks for teachers, students, and the school. In this chapter we identify some of the many purposes for conducting walkthroughs. We will first review the purposes of the more prominent walkthrough models found in today's literature and then review some of the grassroots models developed by individual school districts or schools. As you read this chapter, begin thinking about why you might use walkthroughs. It is essential that your teachers "buy-in" and that the walkthroughs align with your other school improvement initiatives.

The vast majority of classroom walkthrough models are used as tools to evaluate the process of teaching and learning, not to evaluate teachers. According to Pitler and Goodwin (2009, p. 7), "The purpose of a walkthrough is not to pass judgment on teachers, but to coach them to higher levels of performance. Walk-throughs are not teacher evaluations; they are a method for identifying opportunities for improvement and supporting the sharing of best practices across the school."

Information gathered from the walkthrough should become a focus for reflection and dialogue with teachers about instruction, curriculum, and assessment and serves many purposes including:

- providing data for conversations about teaching and learning within professional learning communities;

- collecting data about the school's success in achieving its school improvement goals;
- gathering data on student performance to complement other data about how the students and school are performing;
- determining the alignment of lessons to the curriculum standards;
- identifying practices that are working/not working in the classroom/school;
- assessing professional development needs;
- determining the extent to which the implementation and frequency of new instruction, curriculum, and/or assessment initiatives contribute to improvement in student achievement;
- identifying teachers with strengths in specific areas of instruction, curriculum, assessment, and/or management who can share their expertise with other faculty;
- mentoring or coaching teachers as they assume new positions or assignments;
- creating better rapport with teachers and students through visibility and accessibility.

School Leaders Citing Purposes of Walkthroughs

Walkthroughs take many different forms depending on the purpose of the walkthrough. For some school leaders, the purpose of walkthroughs is to be in touch with what is occurring in their schools on a daily basis. Sharon Weber, a principal in Punxsutawney, Pennsylvania, regularly conducts walkthroughs. They enable her to be aware of what is being taught, how students are responding to various teaching techniques, who are the struggling students, and what to focus on during data and faculty meetings. Weber also sees walkthroughs as a purposeful means to discuss curriculum as well as discipline when talking to parents so they have a more complete picture of their children's educational setting.

For others, the purposes may be more detailed and focused. For Laura Smith, the principal of Heritage Intermediate School in Wentzville, Missouri, the overall purpose is to raise student achievement. Smith utilized data gathered through the Instructional Practices Inventory (IPI) as a focus for collaborative conversations that have led to changes in instructional delivery. The school's teacher team believed that through the continual study of student engagement they would succeed in increasing student learning. Following each data collection day, the school team engaged the collective faculty in well-planned discussions of student engagement. They focused not only on planning student activities, but on how students would actually be engaged in the planned activities.

Mike Carbone, the principal of Kickemuit Middle School in Warren, Rhode Island, has used learning walks to move his teachers away from the "my classroom" mind-set toward seeing the big picture of the whole school reaching high-performing status (Steiny, 2009, p. 31). Carbone has small learning walk teams of teachers observing each other's classrooms guided by questions developed at school-based meetings. Following these walks the entire teaching staff has rich discussions about what is working and is not working and where they must make plans for improving instruction.

Instructional Talk Throughs

Teachers from six different schools in the K-9 Edmonton Public Schools (Alberta, Canada) participate in an on-going classroom-embedded professional development experience known as the *Instructional Talk Throughs (ITT)*. The purpose of ITT is to help teachers move toward effective teacher practice, curricular content, student engagement, and assessment practices that enhance student success. ITT involves each school hosting teacher teams from other schools. The teacher teams visit a selected number of classrooms for 15–20 minutes each. Unique to this process is that observed teachers share in advance what visiting teachers will see and request feedback from the visiting teachers on those observations. Teachers trained to facilitate the ITT process help with the post-observation discussions between hosting teachers and visiting teacher teams (Cronk, et al. 2009).

Robert Miller, the principal of St. Charles East High School in St. Charles, Illinois, works with his administrative team in conducting regular walkthroughs. He sees walkthroughs as a supportive instrument to help with school improvement efforts, particularly focusing on rigor, level of teacher questioning, and student engagement. All administrators who evaluate certified staff participate in this building-wide activity.

Deanne Hillman, Director of Teaching and Learning in Decatur School District #61, Decatur, Illinois, indicates that all principals, assistant principals, and administrators whose duties include curriculum leadership participate in walkthroughs. They are used to maximize the administrator's time in the classroom, provide a vehicle to assess effectiveness of curriculum, and monitor the climate of the school. Furthermore, the walkthroughs help facilitate conversations with staff members about improvements in teaching and learning, and they provide practice in data gathering and reflective thinking. Data from the walkthroughs is used to generate in-depth discussions with the entire building-level staff on instructional strategies and to identify instructional changes that will be made based on the data.

Superintendent James G. Merrill of Virginia Beach City Public Schools, Virginia Beach, Virginia, and his cabinet of administrative leaders conduct learning walks in concert with the school principal and/or assistant principal. Merrill explains that the leadership of the school system must be connected to what goes on in classrooms to better understand the needs of the children, to improve how teachers teach, and to more clearly define what is expected of students and school leaders.

As illustrated by the examples above, some school leaders use walkthrough models developed by an external company or organization while others create their own protocols to best meet their needs.

Walkthrough Models and Purposes

All of the walkthrough models reviewed for this book have the ultimate goal of improving teaching and learning in the classroom. However, models developed by both non-profit and for-profit organizations demonstrate a wide range of practices for reaching that goal. Some models were designed to support a foundation of research on instructional practices found to positively impact student learning. Other models connect more directly with a school desiring a deeper reflective understanding of the results of their instructional and curricular practices on student achievement. In addition, several models have shifted their walkthrough data collection to student behaviors, student responses, and student interviews. In the following sections, we introduce you to these models.

Helpful Idea: Classroom walkthroughs should be used to evaluate instructional and curricular practices, **NOT** people.

Models Based on Research as a Foundation

Research-based models are listed in Figure 3.1: Walkthrough Models and Purposes—Research as a Foundation. All of these models provide professional development opportunities for the staff based on those research-based instructional practices.

The *Learning Walk® routine* was developed at the University of Pittsburgh's Institute for Learning.[1] It is the Institute's signature tool to support a school's systematic focus on instructional improvement. The routine consists of a set of professional activities organized around periodic walks through a school's halls and classrooms using the *Principles of Learning* to focus on the instructional core. The *Principles of Learning* describes instructional practices that enable all students to achieve high academic standards through sustained

Figure 3.1:
Walkthrough Models and Purposes—Research as a Foundation

Model	The Purpose is to:
The Learning Walk® Routine	Inform decisions about professional development based on evidence of teaching and learning and to explore the extent to which new practices and content from professional development have found their way into classrooms.
(McREL) Power Walkthrough™	Observe, evaluate, and record the extent to which teachers are using *Classroom Instruction That Works* strategies, the use of technology by teachers and students, levels of Blooms Taxonomy, evidence of student learning, and other look-fors as required by the district.
Teachscape Classroom Walkthrough (CWT)	Improve student achievement by improving the instructional practices that shape student learning.

and targeted efforts. The purpose of The Learning Walk® routine is to gather evidence of classroom teaching and learning in order to make informed decisions about professional development. Walk participants explore the extent to which new practices and professional development content have been implemented in the classroom, often pinpointing areas for further work. Learning walks are an on-going part of the work of professional learning communities and are always preceded and followed by additional professional develop-

---

[1] The Learning Walk® © 2008 is the property of the Institute for Learning at the University of Pittsburgh and may not be used, reproduced, or distributed without the express written permission of the University of Pittsburgh. The Learning Walk® is a registered trademark of the University of Pittsburgh.

ment opportunities—such as study groups that examine evidence of *student learning* in the classrooms visited.

The *Mid-continent Research for Education and Learning (McREL) Power Walkthrough®* uses McREL research as its foundation. This research led to the publication of *Classroom Instruction that Works: Research-Based Strategies for Increasing Student Achievement* (R. J. Marzano, D. J. Pickering, & J. E. Pollock, 2001) and *Using Technology with Classroom Instruction That Works* (H. Pitler, E. R. Hubbell, M. Kuhn, & K. Malenoski, 2007). The purpose of the Power Walkthrough® is to allow trained observers to observe, evaluate, and use a handheld device to record the extent to which teachers are using *Classroom Instruction That Works* strategies. Results also include information about teacher and student use of technology in the classroom.

The *Teachscape Classroom Walkthrough (CWT)* offers educators a coherent, transparent, and structured process that uses technology-enabled and customizable tools. The ultimate purpose of CWT is to improve student achievement by improving the instructional practices that shape student learning. This process begins by examining student achievement data to identify areas of concern. The walks then focus on collection and analysis of data about classroom practices that impact student achievement. Observers collect and analyze evidence of research-based practices proven effective in improving student achievement. The CWT provides current essential classroom practices to inform comprehensive, data-supported, effective professional development. Through subsequent walks, observers determine the level of implementation of the professional development's featured strategies and the impact of these practices on the improvement of teaching and learning.

Models for Understanding Results of Instructional and Curricular Practices

The protocols designed in some walkthrough models are primarily driven by the school and/or individual teachers examining their practices more deeply and exploring the relationship between local instructional and curricular practices and student performance (Figure 3.2).

The *Bristol Central High School Walk-Through*, Bristol, Connecticut, provides a transparent walkthrough protocol for teachers and other participants. Its purposes are to collect data on the school's instructional effectiveness; provide relevant feedback to teachers, departments, and the school; create a school culture that encourages reflection and dialogue around effective instruction; and to identify professional development needs for each teacher, department, and/or school. Each aspect of the walkthrough contributes to the high school's instructional improvement and, therefore, increases the potential for student learning.

Figure 3.2:
Walkthrough Models and Purposes—
Instructional and Curricular Practices

Model	The Purpose is to:
Bristol Central High School Walk-Through	Collect data on instructional effectiveness; provide relevant feedback to the school; create school culture that encourages reflection and dialogue on effective instruction; and identify professional development needs.
Data-in-a-Day (DIAD)	Provide a short but intensive self-study opportunity for a school interested in gathering and reporting data about issues (themes) that both students and staff have determined as important for school improvement.
Downey Three-Minute Classroom Walk-Through (CWT) with Reflective Practice	Conduct short, focused, informal observations that result in follow-up conversations for reflection, a focus on curriculum and instruction, occasional follow-ups, and an informal and collaborative process.
Hall Walk-Through	Encourage self-reflection, build teacher capacity, and aid in the teacher evaluation process. The model serves a dual utility for developmental and evaluative purposes.
High School Walkthrough	Collect patterns of data on the application to classroom practices of knowledge and skills learned through professional development initiatives.
Instructional Walkthrough	Maintain an awareness of what is going on in classrooms throughout the school and to monitor the progress of specific school initiatives.
Learning Keys' Data Walks	Create a picture of the current reality of instruction in a building.
UCLA SMP Classroom Walk-Through	Help teachers gain a deeper understanding of the results of their current practice and implement the kind of changes to improve practice that improves results.
Walkthrough Observation Tool	See the school in operation and to begin collecting base-line data around a spectrum of effective instructional practices.

Data-in-a-Day (DIAD) is a tool that provides a short but intensive self-study opportunity for a school interested in gathering and reporting data that students and staff view as important for school improvement. The DIAD approach was originally developed by representatives from a national network of Regional Educational Laboratories. This process begins when staff members and/or students identify self-study areas or topics. One school day is designated for data collection and analysis by groups of observers called "research teams." These research teams conduct morning classroom observations and then reassemble over lunch into "analysis groups" that analyze and summarize all observational notes. The analysis groups organize their findings into recommendations and present them to the building faculty and staff at an after-school meeting. By including students as active members of the research teams, the process enables a school to listen to students' voices about their own learning.

The specific purpose of the *Downey Three-Minute Classroom Walk-Through (CWT) with Reflective Practice* is to help teachers learn to reflect proactively on teaching practices before implementing them in the classroom. CWTs are short, informal observations that focus on curriculum and instruction and include time for reflection. More specifically, the protocol looks at curricular and instructional decisions teachers make in the classroom. The Downey CWT has two major parts: the observation and the reflective conversation; it is intended to enable educators to become self-analytical and personally accountable for their work and to encourage educators to work collaboratively.

The *Hall Walk-Through*, created by Pete Hill, the principal at Sheridan Elementary School in Seattle, Washington, is a protocol that encourages self-reflection and builds teacher capacity. Useful "look-fors" are agreed upon during planned, focused conversations between the administrator and the teachers to be observed. Look-fors can come from individual teachers as they set goals relative to their own improvement and expertise; from grade-level teams' instructional goals; or from the entire staff as the means to school improvement. If the look-fors are established building-wide, the administrator will provide both individual and school-wide feedback.

The purpose of the *High School Walkthrough* at Northern High School in Calvert County Public Schools, Prince Frederick, Maryland, is to allow the administrative team to work in instructional areas with teachers in a coaching protocol. According to Principal George Miller, walkthroughs are designed to find patterns that can help members of the professional learning community continually improve their teaching practices (ASCD, 2007).

For Deborah Tyler, principal at Eagle View Elementary School, Fairfax County Public Schools in Falls Church, Virginia, *Instructional Walkthroughs* are snapshots of what is taking place in the classroom. Her primary purposes for conducting them are to maintain an awareness of what is going on in the classrooms throughout the entire school and to monitor the progress of any specific school initiatives.

The *Learning Keys' Data Walks* provide information about classroom instruction, most importantly student engagement and involvement in the learning process. This data can be recorded, stored, and shared in an electronic format to paint a real-time picture of the state of instruction in a school. The model uses a data-driven approach and an electronic format to create research-driven data points. These data points can be quickly and efficiently compiled, disaggregated, and shared with all the members of the learning community to identify needs, measure progress, and set staff development priorities.

> In my school, I see the walkthroughs as a wonderful way to accomplish many different things. For me as a classroom teacher, the walkthroughs serve as a means to continually refine and improve my teaching practices. Knowing that an administrator may be in my classroom to do a walkthrough at any point during the day is a great way to motivate me to always be at my best. For the students, it is good for them to see the principal in a casual manner rather than in just the disciplinary role.
>
> Jodi Bartlebaugh, First Grade Teacher,
> Punxsutawney Area School District, Pennsylvania

A walkthrough model driven by teachers examining their own practices more deeply is the *UCLA School Management Program (SMP) Classroom Walk-Through*. This model links leadership practice to the improvement of instruction in classrooms. It is a learner-focused model that examines directly what can be observed as students are learning. It is a non-evaluative effort to focus on evidence that can connect student learning to the faculty's inquiry about instructional practice. More specifically, the purpose of the UCLA SMP Classroom Walk-Through protocol is to help teachers gain a deeper understanding of the results of their instructional practice and implement the kind of changes needed to garner results. In this model it is teachers who decide what they need to learn to do in order to elicit greater student learning.

The *Walkthrough Observation Tool* is a means for looking at the process of teaching and learning. Developed through the Western Pennsylvania Principals Academy, the purpose of this protocol is to see the entire school as a system in operation and to begin collecting baseline data around a spectrum of effective instructional practices. The walkthrough begins as a process for validating effective teaching practices and sharing successful learning strategies demonstrated by students. The Walkthrough Observation Tool creates an intense focus on specific practices that principals and teachers believe make a difference in how students learn and achieve.

Models That Focus on Student Performance and Opportunities

Some walkthrough models focus specifically on student performance and opportunity (Figure 3.3).

The *Equity Learning Walk*, used in the Kansas City, Kansas Public Schools, responds to such questions as: What does equity look like? Where is evidence of equity? Where are opportunities for increased equity? This observation protocol contains questions about the school and classroom environment; questions about teaching and learning; and questions to ask students during the visit. Observers ask the teachers and students about the content and the objectives of the lesson. Areas of focus include racial, ethnic, and gender diversity, attention to different learning styles, relationships between students and teachers, conveyance of high expectations for all students, availability of resources to support different language learners, and the use of differentiated instruction.

> **Helpful Idea:** If you have a team of observers conducting walkthroughs, strongly consider inter-rater reliability training for sustaining a degree of consistency among observers.

The *Instructional Practices Inventory (IPI) Process* was developed by Jerry Valentine and Bryan Painter in 1996 and refined by Valentine in 2002. The IPI is a practical system for codifying student engagement during instruction. The observer moves from classroom to classroom systematically collecting "snapshots" of student engagement using observation protocols designed to maintain observer accuracy and consistency. The observer then constructs a school-wide profile of engagement on six categories. The overall purpose of the IPI Process is the refinement of instructional practices and related increases in quality student engagement through faculty collaborative study and problelm solving of the data profiles. Building the capacity to grow as a learning community using the IPI data also sets the foundation for collaborative conversations about other issues critical to school improvement and organizational learning.

Figure 3.3:
Walkthrough Models and Purposes—
Student Performance and Opportunities

Model	The Purpose is to:
Equity Learning Walk	Provide a school profile that reveals equity in terms of instruction and opportunities for all students in the school.
Instructional Practices Inventory (IPI) Process	Increase student engagement in meaningful learning by creating school-wide data profiles for collaborative faculty study and problem-solving.
Look 2 Learning (L2L) formerly SMART Walks	Improve student achievement by generating and analyzing data on rigor, relevance, and student engagement. Looking for the *leading indicators* of student achievement in the hands of the learners, the model provides accurate pictures of learning than can be captured by focusing on teacher behaviors.
Mayerson Academy Classroom Walk-Through (CWT)	Develop a learning community focused on improving learning and instruction; involve teachers and principals in a discussion about teaching and learning and meeting the needs of all learners; and provide support for every child in every classroom to meet or exceed high standards.
Palisades School District Walkthrough	Determine district-wide curricular changes and professional development needs by listening to students reveal how they learn, how teachers expect them to learn, and how students believe they could learn better.
School-Wide Walk Through	Unite all instructional staff to observe, discuss, and analyze teaching and learning in order to determine how educators' beliefs shape instructional decisions.

Look 2 Learning (L2L) allows the principal, coaches, or teachers to visit classrooms efficiently, gaining firsthand knowledge of students and their learning experiences. Using data from L2L visits, principals and staff can target professional development to address the areas of greatest need. L2L

incorporates the latest research on student achievement and engagement while honoring accepted, tested research from the past 30 years. The original research base comes from the work of Madeline Hunter, Richard Stiggins, Benjamin Bloom, Larry Lezotte, Douglas Reeves, Robert Mager, Fenwick English, and Robert Marzano. The model incorporates action research conducted in more than 13,000 classrooms by consultants John Antonetti and Jim Garver. The purpose of the L2L is to improve student achievement by generating and analyzing data on rigor, relevance, and student engagement. Rather than focusing on the teachers' classroom practices, L2L captures information about and from the learners. The protocols of data collection include student interviews and analysis of the student work to look at the students' responses to teaching rather than the teaching itself.

Helpful Idea: Some of the richest information about teacher effectiveness during walkthroughs comes from observing and engaging in conversation with students about what they are learning.

The *Mayerson Academy Classroom Walk-Through (CWT)* is an organized visit throughout a school's learning areas. Participants conducting the observations move in and out of classrooms looking at student work and artifacts and talking with students, using a tool that describes student learning. The purpose of CWT is to develop a learning community focused on improving teaching and learning.

The *Palisades School District Walkthrough* in Kintnersville, Pennsylvania, is a district grassroots model designed to gather data beyond what the standardized tests reveal about students and determine more holistically the success of their learning. The district has developed a biannual protocol that assigns teams of educators, parents, and board members to interview all students in the school through one-on-one conversations about what they are learning. The interview questions are created jointly by teachers and administrators and are tailored to the students' general educational level (primary, intermediate, middle, and high school). The purpose of the Palisades School District Walkthrough is to improve the core of educational practice by determining the need for district-wide curricular changes and professional development. Listening to students reveals how they learn, how teachers expect them to learn, and how students believe they could learn better.

The *Penn-Delco School District Walkthrough* is a prime example of a school district developing its own walkthrough process by participating in another district's walkthrough process. Administrators and teachers from Penn-Delco School District, Aston, Pennsylvania, were invited to participate in the walkthroughs at Palisades School District in Kintnersville, Pennsylvania. The value of those experiences resulted in Penn-Delco School District implementing walkthroughs with a focus on looking at student work and talking with students to determine what they could express about their learning. This data-gathering enables building staff to better assess progress toward pre-established goals within each school's or department's Continuous School Improvement Plan. The success at Penn-Delco underscores the value of inviting educators from other schools and districts to be part of walkthroughs. For more information, contact Dr. Alexis McGloin, Assistant Superintendent, Penn-Delco School District at 610-497-6300, ext. 1314 or at amcgloin@pdsd.org.

The grassroots **School-Wide Walk-Through** at James Hubert Blake High School in Silver Spring, Maryland, is a system in which all instructional staff work together to observe, discuss, and analyze teaching and learning in order to determine how educators' beliefs shape instructional decisions. At Blake High School, the walkthrough was designed with the purpose of determining how student motivation is affected by the evidence of personal relationships, classroom climate, high expectations, and literacy support.

In Summary

Walkthroughs contribute significantly to a school's approach to renewal when the purposes are understood by all participants. They are practical and effective for increased dialogue and reflection about teaching practices and are an integral component of a healthy school culture. This chapter demonstrated that although the purposes of walkthrough models vary, they all support an ultimate goal of improvement in teaching and learning. Some models are grounded in the understanding and delivery of research-based instructional practices found to positively impact student learning. Other models provide individual teachers, groups of teachers, or entire school faculties a greater reflective understanding of the impact of their instructional and curricular practices on student results. Still other models focus on student performance and opportunity for engagement, understanding, motivation, and/or equity.

As you reflect on your role as instructional leader in your school, consider the following:

- What are some purposes for conducting walkthroughs that measure and support your efforts to help students succeed?
- How will the purposes of walkthroughs be coordinated with other initiatives designed to improve student achievement in your school?
- How can you assure that everyone is clear as to the purposes of the walkthrough?
- How can walkthroughs be sustained for creating continuous improvement in teaching and learning?

Before launching a walkthrough endeavor in your school, read, study, and explore various walkthrough models to ensure the maximum potential for continuous school improvement. Include a cadre of teachers and other instructional leaders in your exploration.

In Chapter Four, you will see why it is essential to involve teachers in the design, conduct, and evaluation of the walkthrough.

4

Involving Teachers in Classroom Walkthroughs

When planning for walkthroughs in your school, remember the three **Ts** of **T**rust, **T**ransparency, and **T**ruthfulness. Every effort must be taken to build and enhance trust in the relationship between participants visiting classrooms and the teachers being observed. This helps to create a collegial atmosphere and may encourage risk-taking. A key to successful walkthroughs is to keep the entire process transparent from beginning to end. Everyone should know the exact purpose and protocols so that there is no confusion or misunderstanding. Finally, it is important to be truthful about how the walkthrough will be conducted and the data is used. Trust, transparency, and truthfulness are most easily achieved when teachers are involved in all stages of planning. In Chapter 10 we will further explore ways to build trust into the process.

According to Gary Bloom, Associate Director of the New Teacher Center, University of California, Santa Cruz, "It is essential that before a school or district begins a classroom visitation program, everybody is clear about what to expect and what his or her role is to be in the process" (2007, p. 41). Everyone involved needs to know the following 15 items:

1. Why are classroom walkthroughs being considered?
2. What is the purpose of classroom walkthroughs?

3. Who will participate in the walkthroughs?

4. When and how often will walks occur?

5. How long will visitors stay?

6. Will walkthroughs be announced prior to the visit?

7. What focus or look-fors will visitors observe during the walkthrough?

8. Will there be any training connected to the walkthroughs?

9. What information from the visits will be recorded and how will it be used?

10. What will happen to the notes or checklists?

11. How will teachers receive feedback?

12. Will everyone be required to be visited?

13. How will walkthroughs complement other school improvement initiatives?

14. How will walkthroughs relate to the teacher evaluation process?

15. How will the walkthrough process be evaluated and by whom?

Voices from the Field

If walkthrough participants are not faithful to the intent and the protocols set, the process can be useless or even harmful to teachers and students. On the other hand, if participants come into the classrooms equipped with agreed-upon look-fors and a clear understanding of purposes, these brief classroom observations can be powerful tools for promoting excellent teaching (Pitler & Goodwin, 2009, p. 6).

In schools that are highly successful, teachers are involved in every aspect of improvement. They participate in meaningful conversations about how to use data to improve student achievement, and they are central to goal setting for their schools. Although teachers are sometimes reluctant to have "outsiders" in their classrooms, when they are involved in the walkthrough planning process, they are likely to become more receptive. The staff must see walkthroughs as part of the school improvement process and a resource for planning professional development. Walkthroughs are never intended as opportunities for "gotchas."

Helpful Idea: Establish a focus for classroom walkthroughs by working with the teachers in developing the look-fors.

Margery B. Ginsberg and Damon Murphy (2002, p. 35) recommend that administrators and teachers work together to create the walkthrough process that makes sense from everyone's perspective. They also suggest that a time be scheduled to review the process after its initial trial. Teachers and administrators should jointly address the school's approach to walkthroughs by asking a number of questions:

- How can the walkthrough process contribute to our school's approach to renewal?
- What are some reasons for conducting periodic walkthroughs?
- Who should visit classrooms? Which rooms? How often?
- What questions should observers bring to the walkthroughs? What questions should observers ask students?
- What other data can we gather and analyze to complement insights from walkthroughs?
- How can we create a positive experience for all participants?

It is extremely important for all teachers to clearly understand the expectations of what will occur in each classroom. It is the student achievement data and classroom expectations that inform the kind of professional development needed for teachers to build capacity to make necessary adjustments in instruction (Richardson, 2001, p. 2).

Kathy Larson, Staff Development Consultant for the Cooperative Educational Service Agency #2, Milton, Wisconsin, recommends six key steps for conducting classroom walkthroughs (Larson, 2007):

1. Prior to initiating classroom walkthroughs, inform the faculty about the purpose and expectations;
2. Develop district guidelines to sustain district support;
3. Schedule blocks of time for coaching prior to full implementation;
4. Give teachers time to talk about how the process is working;
5. Stay true to the fidelity of the training;
6. Develop learning communities where reflection will be used strategically among the staff.

To ensure that common understanding of walkthroughs exists, former Michigan principal Todd Wiedemann maintains that teachers should be involved in developing the look-fors and listen-fors that are used during the observation as well as the reflective questions that structure the feedback sessions. This joint participation reassures teachers that the walkthrough is a strategy for support, not for evaluation (Center for Comprehensive School Reform and Improvement, 2007, p. 2).

> **Helpful Idea:** Before launching a walkthrough protocol, become acquainted with the literature on walkthroughs and begin with a simple protocol.

Otto Graf recommended a number of steps in planning for the conduct of classroom walkthroughs. He suggested that a preliminary walkthrough be conducted by whoever will be doing the walks. The purpose is to begin collecting baseline data around a wide spectrum of effective instructional practices. That should be followed by a meeting with the staff to establish clear expectations related to the purpose and process of the first walkthrough. Graf next recommends that the focus for walkthroughs should be established by working with teachers to identify the look-fors, the specific elements of effective instruction or guiding principles of learning that they wish to target for implementation. Finally, those look-fors should be connected to the established curriculum standards. This is an important step in developing a common language for staff and for establishing a matching set of indicators around instruction and learning (Protheroe, 2009, pp. 32–33). These steps contribute to the transparency of the process.

Walkthroughs are opportunities for collegial conversations designed to improve student learning, and they require careful planning. The more teachers are involved in the whole spectrum of the walkthrough process, the more trust and support they will have, allowing everyone to benefit.

How Different Models Involve Teachers

Department chairs are active participants in the *Bristol Central High School Walk-Through* in Bristol, Connecticut. The department chairs (all teachers) participate as members of a walkthrough team with an administrator and curriculum specialist. They inform department members as to the timing and types of walkthroughs. Currently the high school is developing a walkthrough structure that teams each department chair with two department members to conduct walkthroughs throughout the building. The protocol requires that after each walkthrough the team discuss what they observed and what they would provide as feedback to the teacher. These conversations encourage walkthrough participants to reflect on the factors involved in excellent instruction.

The *High School Walkthrough* at Northern High School in Prince Frederick, Maryland, is a collegial process. Principal George Miller explained that because of their collaborative planning efforts, teachers recognize that walkthroughs are non-evaluative in nature. Ted Haynie, Director of System Performance for Calvert County Public Schools in Frederick, Maryland, says that walkthroughs are really about opening up classrooms to identify all the good things that are happening. Therefore, teachers are not working in isolation. Instead, they are collaborative problem-solvers with the school improvement team. Walkthroughs also contribute to a job-embedded type of professional development that really leads to high-performing schools and high-performing students (ASCD, 2007).

The focus of *Data-in-a-Day (DIAD)* begins with the school staff members and students identifying self-study areas or topics that will be examined. These are typically extensions of school improvement work already underway. The 24-hour DIAD process begins with an after-school meeting of the teams of observers to identify what will be examined during the data collection day.

DIAD is most effective when the following conditions have been established:

- Staff members participate in the identification of practices to be observed;
- There is a climate of trust in the school;
- The school staff is receptive to the perspective of students and outsiders;

When the ingredients for collaboration are in place, classroom walkthroughs maximize all there is to gain from a professional learning community. Not since graduate school have I had the opportunity to receive and provide feedback with my peers regarding instructional and therapeutic practices. CWTs take advantage of how we all learn best, within the milieu of our day.

Dr. John Frampton, School Psychologist,
Niles Central Day School, Skokie, Illinois

- An established school-based leadership group exists to connect incoming data to ongoing school improvement work;
- The process is tightly connected to the school's improvement work.

The *Downey Three-Minute Classroom Walk-Through (CWT) with Reflective Practice* provides several suggestions for involving teachers in the protocol. Acceptance and success of walkthroughs occur when principals, coaches, and teachers work together to identify the ground rules for the walks before the visits actually begin. Orientation is provided at a regular faculty meeting or a special meeting where the focus of walkthroughs is discussed (Downey et al., 2004, p. 102). Teachers orient students to the fact there will be a walkthrough and that they are not to stop what they are doing. Downey also recommends that parents need to know that administrators are doing walkthroughs so that they will understand why the administrators are not immediately available (p. 104).

Before the *Equity Learning Walk* begins, the school determines areas related to student equity on which they want to focus. Equity walks reflect trust, truthfulness, and transparency through walkthrough agreements made with teachers:

- **Respect:** The walkthrough is a way of honoring the work of the teacher and therefore is not a "gotcha;"
- **Assumption of positive intentions:** Observers approach classroom visits with the assumption that teachers are doing their best work with the best intentions;
- **Collaboration:** All walkthroughs and debriefs are conducted with observers and teachers visited;
- **Openness:** There are no secrets—observers make their work public so everyone can learn together as a community;
- **Honesty:** The observers' descriptions are objective rather than judgmental. It is the role of the principal to use walkthrough data to assist teachers in improving their instruction.

Research in the use of the *Instructional Practices Inventory (IPI) Process* confirms the importance of faculty receptivity to the process. The IPI is most effective in fostering instructional change, deeper engagement, and higher achievement when teacher leaders are the data collectors and share the facilitation of the faculty study of the data with their principals (Valentine, 2007; Valentine & Collins, 2009; Collins, 2009). In many schools, principals are the first to learn about the IPI and attend a workshop. Once the principal is committed to the use of the process, a team of teacher-leaders attend a workshop to develop data-collector reliability and learn about effective strategies for faculty study of the data. Thus, the teacher-leaders and the principal are knowledgeable and can jointly facilitate faculty study and problem solving. Among the strategies designed to encourage transparency and faculty receptivity is the expectation that all staff will be aware of the days when data will be collected. Because that awareness gives rise to the potential for "dog and pony" shows during data collection days, faculty members are asked to reflect on the degree to which they might have "jazzed-it-up" during the data collection period. From those repetitive conversations, an understanding of how the engagement profiles can be skewed and why it is important to proceed with instruction as usual evolves. When teachers own the process, both self-governance and a sustainable, deeper level of change in instructional practices develop.

Pete Hall holds meetings at the beginning of the school year to outline protocols for walkthroughs. In this **Hall Walk-Through** model, the teacher identifies the specific goals to be addressed and then meets with Hall to develop look-fors based on those goals. A group of teachers may have similar goals and thus may work together. At other times, the entire school staff will agree on particular look-fors that relate to the school-wide improvement plan (Hall & Simeral, 2008, pp. 131–132).

Helpful Idea: Establish clear and consistent expectations for the presence of those conducting walkthroughs and communicate those to the entire school community.

In the **Learning Keys' Data Walks** teachers are involved in several ways. First, teacher representatives are invited to the administrative training to implement the program. This allows the teachers to see firsthand what the program is and how it will be used. All teachers view a Learning Keys' Power Point presentation by the building administration explaining the program and allowing for questions and concerns. The data from the walkthroughs is later shared with the entire staff as a means to foster professional conversations and facilitate the planning process.

Professional development about **The Learning Walk® routine** is provided to the entire school staff well in advance of initiating the walks. The Learning Walk® Suite of Tools includes extensive resources for this purpose. The Learning Walk® routine is always related to the professional development in which the staff is already engaged. In most schools, as teachers become more familiar with this protocol, teacher-led walks become more frequent. According to Debra B. Drossner, the principal of Bayard Taylor Elementary School in the School District of Philadelphia, Pennsylvania., "The learning walks are a powerful tool to increase reflective practice; inviting classroom teachers to participate validates their voice as we work hard and work smart to be a best practice achieving school" (D. Drossner, personal communication, August 18, 2009).

With a focus shifting to student behavior, districts are encouraged to not only train teachers in what *Look 2 Learning (L2L)* is all about, but to include teachers in data collection. When teachers are involved from the very beginning of the process and receive their training in tandem with school administrators, the fear of walkthrough-as-evaluation is removed. Likewise, potential misunderstandings about purpose and indicators are greatly reduced. John Antonetti suggests, "After training administrators in many walkthrough models, I've watched them struggle to go back to faculty and try to get *buy-in* to the ideas of walking classrooms. When teachers are involved in the initial training and then help design the implementation, there is no need for *buy-in*; there is already ownership" (J. Antonetti, personal communication, July 20, 2009).

The principal introduces the *Mayerson Academy Classroom Walk-Through (CWT)* with a comprehensive staff orientation so teachers become familiar with the CWT format. Because teachers identify the focus for the walks and the data to be gathered, this model is grounded in a high degree of teacher involvement and trust.

Schools or district-level administrators using the *(McREL) Power Walk-through®* can employ a variety of strategies to inform and involve teachers in this protocol. Because the nine research-based strategies from McREL's *Classroom Instruction That Works* are the foundation for the observations, teachers are prepared through professional development to learn how to implement those strategies in their respective classrooms. They learn what the strategies look like in practice and are informed of when walkthroughs will occur.

The *Palisades School District Walkthrough* model requires teams of educators to engage students in individual conversations about what they are learning. Those teacher leadership teams in each school choose an area to address, and teachers are actively involved in developing specific questions, usually connected to teachers' instruction, to ask of students. The recommendations based on the interviews are teacher-generated; therefore, teachers have a strong investment in following them.

When teachers at James Hubert Blake High School in Silver Spring, Maryland, collaborated to identify the most prevalent problem for their *School-Wide Walk-Through,* the most frequent response was, "Students aren't motivated to succeed!" The school leadership team determined from research that improving student motivation is directly tied to building personal relationships, setting high expectations for all students, creating a positive class climate, and addressing students' literacy needs. The results of the research formed the basis for a semester-long professional development effort. The staff began by identifying their personal beliefs regarding student motivation and writing goal statements reflecting their expectations for their students and their own professional behavior. The staff subsequently defined observable teaching strategies that reflected these beliefs. These strategies/ decisions became the look-fors for the school-wide walkthrough. Ultimately, all staff analyzed the walkthrough data and determined next steps regarding student motivation.

The *Teachscape Classroom Walkthrough (CWT)* involves teachers in a number of meaningful ways.

1. Teachers are provided with resources to familiarize them with the CWT process. These resources include internet-based videos to enable teachers to do a virtual walk; copies of the *CWT* tool for gathering walkthrough data; and discussion ideas about data gathered.

2. Faculty joins with the instructional leaders to reflect on what the data conveys and how they can address the challenges identified.

3. Schools include teachers in developing look-fors and may customize the *CWT* tool to address their specific interests and needs.

4. It is appropriate for faculty to conduct walkthroughs as members of a walking team, as "critical friends," to provide peer support, or to assess the progress of their own application of effective instructional strategies.

Teachers are actively involved with the **UCLA SMP Classroom Walk-Through** protocol. They choose the results they want to influence; they communicate the instructional practices they want to change to improve student learning; and they determine the outcomes that define their success. Before the walk, teachers provide focus questions to guide observations and follow-up conversations. After the walk, all data is presented to the faculty who decides what next steps will be taken to achieve improved student learning.

An initial meeting is held with school staff to introduce the expectations for the *Walkthrough Observation Tool*. Specific school goals, special programs, or areas of focus for the school are reviewed. The principal and teachers work together to identify which elements of effective instruction or guiding principles of learning they wish to target for implementation. They collaboratively develop the look-fors that inform the observer what the strategy actually looks like when applied in the classroom.

In Summary

When classroom walkthroughs are implemented with integrity, the benefits are significant. Results add value to the professionalism of the school culture, instruction improves, and student achievement is increased. Implemented poorly, the process can leave teachers frustrated and distrustful. It is critical to plan thoroughly before beginning a walkthrough protocol and to involve teachers in each step of the planning process to assure Trust, Transparency, and Truthfulness.

As you reflect on your role as instructional leader in your school, consider the following:

- How will teacher involvement benefit the design, implementation, and evaluation of your walkthrough model?
- How might you approach teachers to assist with planning for walkthroughs?
- How do you and staff members address anxiety that teachers experience during walkthroughs?

In Chapter Five, we will turn our attention to individuals who participate as observers in various models of walkthroughs. Depending on the purpose and protocol of the walkthrough, you will learn that many different participants enhance the walkthrough process.

5

Walkthrough Participants and Training

Classroom walkthroughs are often considered a practice of school principals as instructional leaders. As discussed in previous chapters, there is a movement toward shared instructional leadership where the principal is no longer considered the only expert providing all leadership functions.

With increasing frequency, districts and schools are creating new leadership positions such as coach and coordinator—roles that formally expand responsibility for instructional leadership to teachers. As you will learn in this chapter, walkthrough participants include almost everyone in a school's learning community (Figure 5.1). Those involved are district level personnel (superintendent, school board members, curriculum and instruction specialists), building-level administrators and instructional leaders (principals, assistant or associate principals, department chairs, team-level leaders, teacher-leaders, mentors, coaches), collegial participants (teachers, paraprofessionals), and others (educators from outside of the school and school district, parents, community members, and students). Participants are chosen relative to the defined purpose for doing walkthroughs. We believe it is important for school principals to be involved in establishing walkthroughs as a practice in their buildings. Before involving others, principals should acquire a sense of the value of walkthroughs and note challenges that might result for observers and those observed (e.g., timing, teacher anxiety, look-fors, follow-up) during these short visits.

Who Participates in Walkthroughs

In some cases, central office personnel are participants in walkthroughs. Superintendent Terry Holliday of Iredell-Statesville Schools in Statesville, North Carolina, has set a goal to get into building classrooms at least once a week. In addition, he requires central-office administrators in his district to pair with school-level staff to visit classrooms. According to Holliday, the conversations around what is observed in the classrooms have proven to be very powerful learning experiences for both central office staff and building staff.

In Virginia Beach City Public Schools in Virginia Beach, Virginia, administrative teams of two cabinet members are assigned to specific schools and participate in learning walks with the principal and/or assistant principal. Superintendent James Merrill strongly believes that the leadership of his school system needs to be absolutely connected to what is taking place in the classrooms.

> Participating in the walkthrough gave me a great sense of nostalgia experiencing the classroom through the eyes and ears of a child. So often as adults, we forget what it is like to be a child or to think like a child. This view reaffirmed my goals as a classroom teacher.
>
> Leah Perrucci, Teacher, Bayard Taylor Elementary School
> School District of Philadelphia, Philadelphia, PA

Elaine Fink and Lauren B. Resnick wrote about principals walking through a colleague's school. These inter-visitations focused on a specific practice that the visiting leader desired to learn about. For example, one school may be known as excelling in guided reading, or it may be known for pioneering teachers' study groups in mathematics teaching. On such visitations, the principals walk together through classrooms, join staff meetings, and discuss their analysis of the teaching and learning of their subject of interest (Fink & Resnick, 2001, p. 603).

The entire administrative team at Northern High School in Prince Frederick, Maryland, participates in walkthroughs. The administrative team meets twice weekly to examine key elements of instruction relating to staff development. These practices are aimed at increasing student achievement and are expected to be part of each teacher's instruction (ASCD, 2007).

In a variation on this practice, *Look 2 Learning* uses the data collection protocols from the model to provide teachers a process for making these same "exemplar" visits. Principals, coaches, or teachers identify exemplary student learning that the school wishes to replicate in all classrooms. Teachers from other classrooms visit these situations in short rotations. They then process the snapshots of the learning activity into a fully realized picture of what was working at the student level.

Deborah Tyler from Fairfax, Virginia, often teams with a classroom teacher to conduct her instructional walks through the building. Sometimes new teachers accompany her as part of her mentoring process. Other times, she invites teachers who have taken a lead on certain building initiatives to help determine the extent to which those initiatives are being applied in the classroom.

Dr. Otto Graf, a professor at the University of Pittsburgh, recommends grouping *students* to conduct walkthroughs. The student walkthroughs can be organized around a specific content area or grade level or by a general tour of classrooms. Students are asked to identify one strategy they believe promotes better learning and to provide evidence to the teacher. During debriefing, teachers are invited to come listen to the students' observations. Establishing clear expectations for this type of walk is critical. Such expectations might include identifying a specific focus for the observations, using prescribed strategies for collecting data, and establishing procedures for confidentiality and giving feedback. According to Graf, the student walkthrough is an important piece in opening the instructional environment of the school to all stakeholders.

In Newport News Public Schools, Newport News, Virginia, Michael Evans, former principal at Denbigh High School, used students to conduct walkthroughs. The students were equipped with the same forms given to staff when peer walkthroughs were conducted. Students were given specific areas to focus on during this experience and were given time to share their reflections at a faculty meeting. The open, honest dialogue was non-threatening because teachers' names were not shared. During the content team meetings, lead instructors were able to begin conversations with teachers. For more information, contact Michael Evans, Executive Director of Secondary Education at 757-591-4647 or at michael.evans@nn.k12.va.us.

Walkthrough Models Requiring Formal Training

Walkthroughs should not be introduced to a school until there has been adequate preparation on the part of the school leaders. That preparation can be through individual study of classroom walkthrough literature or attendance at workshops, seminars, or institutes on walkthroughs. Education groups, including professional development companies, professional associations, colleges and universities, and intermediate educational agencies are sources to consider for classroom walkthrough training.

A number of established models for walkthroughs require that participants be trained in the content and protocols of the respective model and know how to customize protocols to meet their specific school/district needs (Figure 5.1). Companies and organizations that sponsor walkthrough models provide training at their offices as well as at school or district sites.

School staffs using the *Downey Three-Minute Classroom Walk-Through (CWT) with Reflective Practice* model decide who participates as the observers. In many cases, it will be the principal although it could include any other educators in a supervisory role such as a department chair or coach. It could be the principal observing with other teachers and/or peers visiting each other's classrooms. The primary emphasis of the Downey Three-Minute Classroom Walk-Through is the collaborative, reflective dialogue between observers and teachers that follows classroom visits. It is critical that all participants be trained to conduct collaborative, thoughtful, and reflective interactions with teachers.

The primary data collectors for the *Instructional Practices Inventory (IPI) Process* should be teacher-leaders. In some cases, principals, central office staff, leaders from regional educational agencies, and occasionally personnel from other schools share in the data collection process. Data collectors are required to receive formal workshop training in the IPI Process and attain a rating of .80 or higher on the inter-rater reliability assessment at the conclusion of the workshop. Observers thus become "certified" IPI coders with permission to conduct data collection, build student engagement profiles, and facilitate faculty study of the profiles. Teacher-leaders, working in their own schools, are clearly the most appropriate data collectors and facilitators of the study of IPI data profiles.

Helpful Idea: Provide professional preparation for both teachers and administrators about the classroom walkthrough approach.

All administrative personnel within the district or building participate in the data-gathering portion of the *Learning Keys' Data Walks*. All building instructional staff are observed and included in the data on classroom instruction and student engagement and involvement in the learning process; all administrative and instructional staff reviews the data. The staff then uses that data to identify needs, measure progress, and plan appropriate staff development. Learning Keys provides school-site training for participants to practice and reflect on the process of conducting school-wide classroom visits.

Participants in *The Learning Walk® routine* vary according to the learning needs of the participants and/or of the school staff. Typically, it is the school principal who introduces learning walks, although they may be led by other administrators or teacher-leaders. By definition, this learning walk is a team effort. Participants such as coaches or teacher-leaders often assume school leadership roles as The Learning Walk® routine becomes an established part of the school's learning community focus. Participants receive training in the use of The Learning Walk® routine from the Institute for Learning at the University of Pittsburgh.

For the *Look 2 Learning (L2L)* model, the shift to student behavior rather than teacher behavior requires a rather formalized training schedule conducted for the schools by trainers from Colleagues on Call. Principals, instructional coaches, and classroom teachers participate in an initial day-long training of "learning 2 look" in which exemplars of the look-fors are presented in video vignettes. After the exemplar of each component is analyzed and distilled to its critical elements, the trainees move into live classrooms in groups of five to look for that particular component. As the training continues, the teams add one component at a time until the entire set of look-fors becomes the protocol for data collection in the live classrooms at the end of the day. Training must be done at a school site with access to multiple classrooms. The follow-up training focuses on the reflective processes and tools for understanding and acting on the information garnered in L2L visits. Thus, the goal is "looking to learn" from the data collection. To assure that trend data is reliable, training teams work for six weeks practicing their data collection and working toward inter-rater reliability before they attend the second full day of training.

In the Greenville County Schools, Greenville, South Carolina, Associate Superintendent Katherine H. Howard began the process of training all levels of school principals in best practice classroom instructional strategies. Using these strategies, the district's teaching and learning team developed a walkthrough instrument for the purpose of classroom instructional supervision for use by all school principals. The instrument is based on the extensive training of all teachers in effective teaching practices. All district principals were trained in appropriate observation skills for improving classroom instruction using this tool. Before use in the classroom, principals presented the walkthrough process to teachers, a very important part of this process. The walkthrough is also used by the district's teaching and learning team, led by the associate superintendent. Hard evidence of walkthroughs is now required of principals by their immediate supervisors for principal portfolio evaluations. The walkthroughs have proven to be a way of effectively monitoring classroom instructional practices and improving student achievement. For more information, contact Katherine H. Howard, Associate Superintendent, at 864-355-3188 or at kahoward@greenville.k12.sc.us.

In the *Mayerson Academy Classroom Walk-Through (CWT)*, observers move through the school's instructional areas to focus on collecting data on student learning. While the principal alone *can* walk through, teachers, coaches, counselors, central office administrators, and/or board members frequently move in and out of classrooms looking at student work. Involvement of other stakeholders in the school setting contributes to the efforts to develop and build a learning community focused on improving learning and instruction. Training on the Classroom Walk-Through protocols is offered by the Mayerson Academy.

Participants in the *(McREL) Power Walkthrough*® model usually include school and district administrators and curriculum directors. McREL participants must demonstrate a thorough understanding of the nine categories of instructional strategies in McREL's research on *classroom instruction that works*. This training requires a two-day seminar offered by the Mid-continent Research for Education and Learning (McREL) at their offices or on-site at the school, district, or intermediate agency location. Using McREL's Power Walkthrough software, participants learn how to observe, evaluate, and record their observations on handheld devices. Observations relate effective instructional strategies, student engagement, and teachers' use of technology that influence student learning.

Helpful Idea: Consider inviting teachers and administrators from other schools in your district to join with your teachers in conducting team walkthroughs.

The intent of classroom walks (e.g., identify professional development needs, measure implementation of a new initiative, enhance peer coaching) determines the participants in the *Teachscape Classroom Walkthrough (CWT)*. The walkthroughs are usually conducted by instructional leaders— principals, assistant principals, department heads, coaches, and lead teachers. At the discretion of the school or district, other professionals may conduct the walks. The CWT may include any participants who have been identified by the instructional leaders and who have been trained to implement the walkthrough process with fidelity. Participants may, for example, include additional instructional leaders, district staff, and, if appropriate, parents and students. Like the McREL model, training is provided to participants on research-based classroom practices proven effective in improving student achievement, how to identify those practices through walks, and how to record observations using Teachscape software on a handheld device.

Classroom teachers are the primary participants both as observers and as classroom hosts for the students being observed in the *UCLA School Management Program (SMP) Classroom Walk-Through*. Their direct involvement promotes school-wide discussions on instructional practices and student performance. In some school situations, administrators, parents, and external consultants may be invited to join teachers in this endeavor. This walkthrough can address instructional needs for grade levels or departments. This model with training provided relies on a teacher-led process and offers teachers the physical space and freedom to collaborate in learning. It is left up to a school's instructional staff to determine if or when the principal can participate as one of the walkthrough team members.

The school principal is the primary trained observer conducting the *Walkthrough Observation Tool*. While the process begins with the principal and other administrators, including teachers in the walkthrough can be an excellent opportunity for all school participants to talk about instruction and learning and to coach one another. This model also provides for students to be walkthrough participants.

Figure 5.1:
Participants in Walkthrough Models as Observers

Models Requiring Formal Training	Participants Who Observe
Downey Three-Minute Classroom Walk-Through (CWT) with Reflective Practice	In some cases, it is the principal. In other cases, it could be the principal with other teachers or coaches, mentors, and/or peers visiting each other's classrooms.
Instructional Practices Inventory (IPI) Process	IPI data collection is best conducted by teacher-leaders in their respective schools. In some instances, principals, central office staff, and others may serve as data collectors. Those using the IPI Process are required to be "certified" to collect data and facilitate faculty study of the data.
Learning Keys' Data Walks	All administrative personnel within the district or building participate in the data-gathering portion of the Data Walks.
The Learning Walk® Routine	Participants vary according to the learning needs of the school staff. Walks may be led by administrators or teacher-leaders. When learning walks are first introduced, the leader is usually the school principal.
Look 2 Learning (L2L) formerly SMART Walks	Participants may include any persons involved in instructional design or delivery in a school. Administrators are encouraged to include classroom teachers, coaches, and union representation at the initial training.
Mayerson Academy Classroom Walk-Through (CWT)	The walks involve principals and teachers and may include counselors, central services, and board members.
(McREL) Power Walkthrough®	Participants usually include school and district administrators and curriculum directors. They may also include teachers.
Teachscape Classroom Walkthrough (CWT)	While this varies according to the intent of the walks, walkthroughs are usually conducted by instructional leaders. At the discretion of the school or district, other professionals may conduct the walks.

UCLA SMP Classroom Walk-Through	Classroom teachers themselves are the primary participants of the walkthroughs: the visitors and the subject of the visits.
Walkthrough Observation Tool	The school principal is the primary observer. Other administrators and teachers can be observers as well.
Models NOT Requring Formal Training	**Participants Who Observe**
Bristol Central High School Walk-Through	The principal, assistant principals, department chairs, district curriculum coordinators, department chairs, and teachers may do the walks.
Data-in-a-Day (DIAD)	Each research team is comprised of a parent, teacher, and student. In a school with 36 classrooms, 12 teams would visit three classrooms each.
Equity Learning Walk	This model uses a team—principal, instructional coach, teachers, others—to conduct building walk-throughs to examine the school's efforts to close the achievement gap and teach all students equitably.
Hall Walk-Through	Walkers include the school administrators or supervisors responsible for the development and evaluation of teachers.
High School Walk-through	The high school's whole administrative team (principal and assistant principals) participates in the walkthroughs.
Instructional Walk-through	The observer is often the school principal alone or teamed with classroom teachers in the walkthrough.
Palisades School District Walkthrough	Walkthrough interviewing teams are composed of the district's own educators, volunteers, parents, and school board members as well as educators from other schools, districts, and higher education.
School-Wide Walk-Through	Every teacher in the high school is part of a visiting team. Teams are composed of four people. Each team member represents a different department, teaches at a different level, and has a different amount of experience from the other team members.

Walkthrough Models Not Requiring Formal Training

A number of the walkthrough models reviewed for this book do not require specific training. However, some preparation is necessary for participants in conducting a walkthrough, even if it is not offered in formally held seminars or workshops. Participants need a common understanding of what they are looking for as well as expected protocols for professional courtesy. The intent is to assure that walkthrough data is based on consistent evidence of practices that can be useful for future planning.

The *Bristol Central High School Walk-Through* has been evolving, and as a result, the makeup of the participants has changed over time. During the first year, each member of the administrative team (one principal and two assistant principals) conducted ten classroom walkthroughs each week. The administrative team developed a protocol for team walkthroughs. It provided feedback to each teacher observed, but more importantly, promoted conversations among the walkthrough team. These conversations occurred after each walkthrough and focused on what was observed. The team also decided on feedback provided to the teacher based on walkthrough data. In each case the team was provided with an opportunity to discuss what constitutes excellent instruction and how to improve instruction. In subsequent years, department chairs and district curriculum coordinators have been involved. Twice a year an administrator, curriculum coordinator, and department chairs team up to complete group walkthroughs. As this process continues to evolve, each department chair will be asked to conduct classroom walkthroughs with two members of the department and follow the developed protocol.

The *Data-in-a-Day (DIAD)* model begins with the selection of a design team to coordinate the work at the school. Staff members and/or students identify self-study areas in or topics for which they want to gather information. This team's responsibilities fall into two categories: (1) establishing a connection between DIAD and the school's improvement work; and (2) coordinating the logistics of the data collection day. One of the logistical responsibilities is to recruit and select members of research teams (each made up of a teacher, parent, and student). Students who are articulate and thoughtful make good DIAD researchers. These student-adult teams visit a sample of classrooms and record specific examples of classroom or school activities that embody the identified areas for study and improvement. Although this model does not require training, it is recommended that a skilled facilitator be recruited to prepare the school staff, to orchestrate the process, and to provide an orientation to the research teams.

The *Equity Learning Walk* model involves a team of educators examining the school's efforts to close the achievement gap and teach all students equitably. This protocol is designed to be used collaboratively by a team that includes the principal, instructional coach, teachers, and others. Participants receive a copy of the *Observation Guide for Equitable Classroom Practices*, developed by The Education Alliance at Brown University, featuring the qualities of each look-for by describing specific observable behaviors that communicate equitable classroom practices.

Helpful Idea: Invite teachers to observe other teachers through walk-throughs so that collaborative, reflective conversations can become commonplace.

Principal Pete Hall sees the *Hall Walk-Through* as primarily his responsibility as the supervisor and evaluator of teachers. Hall notes that these visits provide abundant opportunities for a school administrator to see what is really taking place throughout the building in the areas of instruction, curriculum, and classroom management. The administrator is then responsible for follow-up conversations with teachers that enable them to reflect on their own professional growth.

ASCD offers *How to Conduct Effective High School Walkthroughs* (2007), a DVD on the *High School Walkthrough* model. The principal and assistant principals participate in weekly administrative staff meetings to discuss the planned walkthroughs and their results. Teachers and department chairs may be invited to participate as well.

ASCD also features a DVD, *How to Conduct Effective Classroom Walkthroughs* (2006) for the *Instructional Walkthrough* model. The school principal is the primary person conducting walkthroughs, although classroom teachers can be invited to participate. Those chosen can be new teachers, teacher-leaders, teacher team leaders, and paraprofessionals. Both DVDs provide a sound overview of walkthroughs and can be very helpful for introducing the concept.

In the *Palisades School District Walkthrough* model, the superintendent invites a wide range of participants to serve on interview teams. The first Palisades walkthrough teams were comprised of the district's own educators, volunteers, parents, and school board members. In later years, educators including superintendents and assistant superintendents from other districts were invited to join district staff along with higher education representatives. Many of those participants subsequently encouraged their own district principals and teachers to volunteer. Superintendent Francis Barnes believes that by inviting outside teams, value is achieved in two ways: as educators, these people can both share good ideas from their districts and spread news about the good work of the Palisades School District students and staff (Barnes and Miller, 2001).

> The walkthroughs that we did at our school were very helpful. Each teacher was able to see classes from many different levels and subject areas. The time built in to discuss what our walkthrough team saw was extremely beneficial. In addition, the after school voluntary school-wide discussion provided the opportunity for the entire staff to discuss how to improve teaching in our school. We were able to celebrate many of our successes, but also have some good discussions about what we need to improve on as a school.
>
> Jeff Newby, Social Studies Resource Teacher
> James Hubert Blake High School, Silver Spring, Maryland

At James Hubert Blake High School, staff development teacher Moriah Martin reports that every teacher in the school is part of a visiting team of their *School-Wide Walk-Through*. Teams are usually comprised of four teachers, each representing a different department, different level, and different years of experience from other team members. Each team is assigned three or four classrooms that are varied by level and subject and are in close proximity to one another. Because every teacher in the school serves on a visiting team and is visited by a team, the entire instructional staff is able to discuss, analyze, and learn about common areas that are the focus of the visits.

In Summary

Walkthrough models reviewed in this chapter demonstrate that all stakeholders in the school's learning community may be considered as participants in the process. The need for appropriate training and preparation of those who will do the walkthroughs varies with the model and purpose of the walkthrough. Everyone should have a common understanding of the focus of the walks, how to observe and record data, and how to provide feedback. Training assures a common understanding of the look-fors.

As you reflect on your role as instructional leader in your school, consider the following:

- Who might you involve as part of your school walkthroughs?
- For what purposes might you involve others in walkthroughs?
- What kind of preparation is needed for those who will conduct these walkthroughs?

The use of frequent, quick, and informal visits to classrooms conveys to the teachers the high expectations of school leaders for excellent instruction and improved student learning. A significant result of walkthroughs is to engage teachers in professional dialogue and reflection about instructional practices and student learning.

You can use the references in this book to further explore the classroom walkthrough as a tool. Appendix A summarizes all of the models discussed in this book and includes contact sources for further information. Appendix B provides a comparative display of all of the models. Appendix C is a template for you to design your own school or district walkthrough model.

In Chapter Six, we will examine various protocols used in classroom walkthroughs to demonstrate the numerous decisions to be made while designing an effective walkthrough process for your school.

6

Classroom Walkthrough Protocols

In previous chapters we have covered varieties of purposes for classroom walkthroughs, the range of participants in walkthroughs, and different kinds of look-fors used during walkthroughs. In this chapter, we will present a variety of protocols or ways walkthroughs are conducted, including guidelines for walkthroughs and such factors as number of observers, length and frequency of visits, and announced or unannounced visits. As we have maintained throughout the book, decisions about walkthroughs are always related to their purpose. As you read this chapter, think about decisions you need to make to meet the needs of your school.

Guidelines for Walkthroughs

There should be clear guidelines for all participants in the walkthrough as suggested by Otto Graf and Joseph Werlinich, professors at the University of Pittsburgh. Expectations concerning the professional behaviors for individuals participating in the walkthrough must be well established. Participants must maintain the highest degree of confidentiality regarding what is observed in the classrooms. Whenever a teacher or school has particular needs or requests, this information should be communicated prior to the walkthrough itself. To assure the value of the walkthrough process, it is important to assure two-way communication (Graf & Werlinich, 2002, p. 10).

Data-in-a-Day guidelines include (1) watching quietly while observing; (2) locating an unobtrusive place to sit and observe; (3) showing respect for teachers and students during and after your visit; and (4) acting in a way that will minimize impact on student learning. These guidelines are appropriate for all walkthrough models.

Deborah Tyler emphasizes in her *Instructional Walkthroughs* the importance of being unobtrusive and positioning oneself initially out of the way, possibly at the back of the room. If walkthrough participants will interview students, it is important that teachers know in advance that it will happen and only when direct instruction is not occurring. Ginsburg and Murphy suggest that observers should walk the entire room. They recommend that a good memory device is to physically touch the back wall of each classroom visited (2002, p. 36).

When an individual makes a classroom visit during the *Look 2 Learning (L2L)*, that person is encouraged *not* to stay at the back of the room, which tends to force a focus on the teacher. Rather, the visitor is trained to go to a front corner of the room to be able to see students' faces and watch as they respond and interact with the instructional design. The visitor then randomly chooses a student for a short interview about the objective, specifics of the activity, and relevance of the learning task. While this is uncomfortable for classroom teachers initially, they recognize the value of the interview from conducting walkthroughs themselves.

Although participants may engage students in brief conversations, the *Mayerson Academy Classroom Walk-Through (CWT)* reminds us that when there is a team of observers in a classroom, they do not talk with one another as this can be an added distraction. Also, observers should remember to turn off their cell phones during the walkthroughs.

For the *School-Wide Walk-Throughs* at James Hubert Blake High School, teams of teachers visiting classrooms are asked to record actual quotes from a teacher or student rather than paraphrasing. In addition, they are to refrain from making judgmental comments during the walkthroughs; not hold conversations with one another while in the classroom, and save discussion until the debriefing.

Number of Observers in a Classroom

While in some models only one person (usually an administrator or coach) conducts the walkthrough, other models use a team of observers, finding that team observations are more comprehensive and provide more data points for discussion. Too many observers can be distracting, so the number must be carefully considered when planning.

> **Helpful Idea:** When a team of observers from outside of your school participates in walkthroughs, provide them a map of the school to help them locate classrooms and organize and track their classroom visits.

Lynnette Harris, Middle School SOL Coordinator for Fairfax County Public Schools, Fairfax, Virginia, reports that they have had as many as six people on the walks in the same classroom without undue distraction. Harris believes the major point to consider is the culture in the building or district. Once the culture includes people in and out of classrooms, even students become quite comfortable with visitors and with people asking them questions (L. Harris, personal communication, July 13, 2009).

Length and Frequency of Walkthroughs

We defined walkthroughs early on as brief, focused classroom visits. A determining factor for the actual length of walkthroughs is their frequency. Seeing walkthroughs as snapshots of what is taking place in the classroom means that the more snapshots, the clearer the picture. For example, completing walkthroughs in 15 classrooms a day for 10 minutes each would take a minimum of two and one-half hours to complete. Completing walkthroughs in 15 classrooms for four minutes each would take a minimum of one hour. It would be easier to get in more visits at the shorter amount of time and capture more snapshots of what is taking place in those settings. Visits range from what Pete Hall and Alisa Simeral call "rounds" (2008, p. 126) that last 30–45 seconds to the *Data-in-a-Day* model that calls for up to 20 minutes. According to Downey, a three-minute walk is adequate. Even this short time span can allow the observer to view something that might be useful for the teacher to reflect upon later (2004). Refer to Figure 6.1 for the recommended amount of time for visits according to various walkthrough models. Keep in mind that the amount of time also relates to the focus of the walkthrough.

> **Helpful Idea:** Attach a digital timer to your notebook or clipboard and set the number of minutes you want to remain in the classroom.

Several considerations have to be reviewed relating to frequency. If walk-throughs are meant to be an integral part of your school's culture, they should occur on a regular, consistent basis. The frequency according to the *UCLA SMP Classroom Walk-Through* is determined by what the school has as its purpose for the walkthrough. Thus, the walkthrough can be daily, weekly, or monthly. However, for the *Data-in-a-Day* and the *Palisades School District Walkthrough*, the walkthroughs are conducted only twice, once in the fall and again in the spring. The fall walkthrough data is used as the basis for the school to create a school improvement plan that will be implemented and later assessed by a walkthrough in the spring.

Figure 6.1:
Length of Observation Time for Walkthrough Models

Model	Observation Minutes
Bristol Central High School Walk-Through	5–10
Data-in-a-Day (DIAD)	20
Downey Three-Minute Classroom Walk-Through	2–3
Equity Learning Walk	10
Hall Walk-Through	5–15
High School Walkthrough	2–5
Instructional Practices Inventory (IPI) Process	1–3
Instructional Walkthrough	5–10
Learning Keys' Data Walks	3–4
The Learning Walk® Routine	5–25
Look 2 Learning (L2L) (formerly SMART Walks)	4
Mayerson Academy Classroom Walk-Through (CWT)	5–10
(McREL) Power Walkthrough®	3–5
Palisades School District Walkthrough	15
School-Wide Walk-Through	7–10
Teachscape Classroom Walkthrough (CWT)	4–7
UCLA SMP Classroom Walk-Through	5–7
Walkthrough Observation Tool	5

Ted R. Haynie in the Calvert County Public Schools, promotes a walk-through method he calls "5 by 5." The administrator plans to visit five classes per day for five minutes each, and he/she should write down five different pieces of information collected (ASCD, 2007). Of course, you can vary that method and do a "3 by 3" or "4 by 4," but find a number and frequency that keeps the process simple and manageable for you.

Kim Marshall, consultant and author of the Marshall Memo, a weekly newsletter summarizing educational research and ideas, indicates that the key to maintaining frequency of short visits is to set a target for the average number of visits per day and be diligent in reaching that daily goal (2009, p. 24). The priorities of administrators shift, so some days are more opportune for walkthroughs. When they are scheduled on the master calendar and are not left to chance, it is more likely that they will be completed and that their importance will be conveyed.

According to Deborah Tyler of Fairfax, Virginia, adequate walkthrough frequency can be best measured when they are such a part of the school culture that instruction continues without interruption, and neither students nor teachers are distracted by visitors.

John Antonetti and Jim Garver have found that in terms of their impact on school improvement, walkthroughs should be conducted in every classroom every other week. In other words, maximum growth occurs when all classrooms involved in the improvement plan (i.e., increasing reading scores in third grade) are walked "randomly" twice per month during the appropriate instructional block (J. Antonetti, personal communication, July 20, 2009).

Regardless of the model you choose, the goal should be to establish a number of walkthroughs that you can realistically achieve. If you are unable to meet your initial goal of visiting every classroom once a week, we recommend that you change that goal to visit every classroom once every two weeks, or once a month. You can always visit more often if your schedule permits, but do not set a goal so high that you will not be able to accomplish what you had planned.

Announced Versus Unannounced Walkthroughs

An understandably debatable issue is whether walkthroughs should be announced in advance or should be conducted as unannounced events. Several issues have to be considered before giving an answer. What is the purpose of the walkthrough? What is the culture of comfort and trust within that school setting? How have teachers and walkthrough participants been prepared for and involved in the planning for walkthroughs? If the teacher is not aware of what the observer is looking for during the walkthrough, it doesn't matter whether the walks are announced or unannounced. The anxiety, intimidation, and even fear will be apparent among many teachers. Remember the importance of trust, truthfulness, and transparency when making these decisions.

Addie Hawkins, Director of Equity for the Kansas City, Kansas Public Schools, suggests that the time and date of each walkthrough should be announced in advance. She knows she is not there to evaluate teachers but to learn and listen to teachers and students. Hawkins and the host team engage in conversations concerning evidence of equitable/inequitable classroom practices and offers suggestions for improvement.

According to David Cohen, Principal of Midwood High School in Brooklyn, New York:

> As long as the walkthrough process is never confused or overlapped with evaluation/assessment, I think the idea of announced or unannounced becomes less significant. I think that the question of announced vs. unannounced is another way of asking how can we make teachers trust the process of learning through professional learning communities. (D. Cohen, personal communication, May 21, 2009)

Figure 6.2 highlights the difference between announced and unannounced walkthroughs:

Figure 6.2:
Announced versus Unannounced Walkthroughs

Announced	Unannounced
• avoids appearance as a "gotcha" approach to classroom visits	• determines if expected curricular, instructional, and/or assessment practices are actually being implemented in the classroom
• enables teachers to demonstrate the very best in practices	• acquires a more authentic view of what is occurring in the classroom
• develops a sense of professional trust and relationships	• reduces staged lessons
• focuses on areas of needed attention for professional growth	• focuses on areas of needed attention for professional growth
• reduces anxiety or intimidation of staff not accustomed to classroom walkthroughs	• encourages compliance by sending message that a visitation can occur at any time

In a school culture where trust and professional confidence are norms, walkthroughs—announced or not—provide data for conversations about how to improve teaching and increase student learning.

Data Recording and Follow-up

How—or whether—data is recorded during a walkthrough depends on the model. Although most models provide for immediate documentation in order to facilitate meaningful follow-up, they range from requiring no written documentation to the use of checklists or even detailed narrative recording of observations. Richardson (2001, p. 3) adds that observers might want to sketch out a map of the classroom during observations in order to indicate the location of evidence of what they observed.

The comfort level of the teacher can be negatively affected by an observer taking notes during a walkthrough, whether writing on a clipboard or entering information on a PDA. For that reason, the *Instructional Walkthrough, UCLA SMP Classroom Walk-Through,* and *Instructional Practices Inventory (IPI) Process* all require observers to follow observation codes and make notes of, and/or discuss their observations outside of the classroom immediately following the walkthrough. However, because it is essential to remember events with accuracy, notes are usually necessary to allow for meaningful follow-up conversations with teachers.

Helpful Idea: If there are multiple observers in the same classroom, assign each observer a different task: timekeeper, talking with students, noting what is displayed on the walls, or watching a specific teaching strategy.

Most walkthrough models suggest that there be some kind of follow-up to teachers after walkthroughs. Downey suggests that follow-up occur only occasionally rather than after every visit (2004, p. 3). Because walkthroughs are frequent, short snapshots of what is taking place in the classroom, the follow-up conversation can have more value with several snapshots or walkthroughs clustered together. On the other hand, Kim Marshall (2009, p. 25) cites the fact that all teachers, including superstars, are hungry for feedback. When he had served as a principal, he made it his business to follow up with every teacher he observed within 24 hours.

The best form of follow-up to teachers depends on the purpose of your walkthroughs, the nature of the data, and the agreed-upon protocols. Follow-up is usually given individually, but combined data is useful for decisions made by grade-level teams, departments, or the whole school. As with most formative data in coaching, mentoring, and teacher evaluation, the closer to the walkthrough the "fresher" the information will be. The follow-up and subsequent conversations should occur within 24–48 hours.

Some administrators use hand-written notes, e-mail, post-it notes, and checklists for their follow-up. Others believe that follow-up should only be given in face-to-face communication that can occur virtually anywhere—outside the principal's office or in the teacher's classroom, hallway, parking lot, teachers' lounge or while walking with the teacher to or from a meeting. Downey believes that notes as a form of follow-up are just a one-way form of communication. They convey in her terms, "adult-child communications—*bosslike*." She feels it reinforces a hierarchical relationship rather than the professional collaborative interaction she desires (2004, p. 46). Rather than feedback, Downey prefers to have a follow-up nonjudgmental conversation with a teacher after a number of visits rather than after each visit.

The *Look 2 Learning (L2L)* model also discourages individual feedback to a teacher after a single visit. Antonetti and Garver find that the teacher's dependence on the administrator for feedback serves to further the idea that the walks are evaluative. Antonetti suggests that "teachers do not want feedback—they want validation" (J. Antonetti, personal communication, July 20, 2009). If we give a teacher feedback after a single visit, walkthroughs become perceived as a system for either praising or fixing teachers. From the inception, L2L postpones the feedback loop until there is valid trend data about a group of learners and the instruction they receive. This trend data may be garnered at a grade level, across a discipline, or across the entire school. All teachers involved in this instruction then become involved in the initial analysis of the trend data and the subsequent development of an action plan.

Other Walkthrough Protocols

When you commit to making walkthroughs a significant part of your school/district improvement efforts, it is essential to schedule inviolate time for them. Because of an overload of administrative tasks it may be tempting to relegate them to the bottom of an endless list of management and crisis issues that constantly compete for your time. To benefit student achievement, however, some administrators use reminder techniques to help keep walk-throughs a priority. One principal created a screensaver flashing the word "walkthrough" to remind him. A mentor reminded himself of walkthroughs by scheduling them on his daily calendar like any other meeting. In a school district, central office administrators were advised of "sacred" walkthrough time of principals at the building levels, and those administrators were asked to respect it. Another principal made it her practice to hand-deliver daily announcements (rather than issuing them from her office) as a means for walking through classrooms.

When scheduling walks, visits by subject level or grade level work well. Walking through classrooms at different times gives a good overall perspective of each room. This also provides an opportunity to observe the beginning, middle, and closure of a lesson or class. We also recommend varying the walks so that both morning and afternoon classes are visited.

The *Instructional Practices Inventory (IPI) Process* calls for multiple observations during the year taking place on "typical" school days when no unusual circumstances that disrupt the normalcy of the data collected. It is also an IPI protocol to collect observational data only on Mondays through Thursdays, avoiding Fridays unless the faculty determines that a Friday data collection would provide valuable insights (Valentine, 2007, p. 5). In the Northern Lights School Division No. 69, Bonnyville, Alberta, Canada, walkthroughs are completed for each teacher weekly except for the months of December and June. December is the month dedicated to the Christmas concerts/holiday season and June for the provincial achievement tests.

There are several ways of letting teachers know when you are entering the classroom for a walkthrough. George Miller at Northern High School in Calvert County, Maryland, asks that his administrative team use clip-boards with the word, "WALKTHROUGH" printed on the back and hold the clipboard with the word exposed so teachers and staff know that the administrator is doing a walkthrough (ASCD, 2007). In Aurora East School District (Illinois) a negotiated union item stated that observers must make it clear to the teacher that a classroom walkthrough is taking place by wearing a "snapshot" pouch or by another agreed-upon signal such as carrying a notepad, wearing a badge, button, or colored clothing item, or nodding silently.

In the hectic workday of an administrator, it is helpful to keep record of walkthrough visits. See Figure 6.3 as a sample of recording walkthroughs (Zepeda, 2007, p. 74). This information can be recorded in the daily planner, on a PDA, or on a computer.

Figure 6.3:
Recordkeeping Template

Teacher	Observer	Walkthrough Visits	Date of Follow-Up	Period(s)/ Times(s)	Follow-Up Topics
Ottoman	Johnson	10/01/2009 11/07/2009	10/02/2009 11/09/2009	8:30–9:15 am 10:00–10:45 am	Differentiated Instruction (e-mail) Classroom Management (hallway conversation)

In Summary

In earlier chapters we addressed the research on walkthroughs, the varied purposes of walkthroughs, and who might participate, including teachers. As illustrated in this chapter, we examined numerous decisions that need to be made in preparation for a walkthrough. Even the smaller decisions like how many visitors, length of time for visits, when visits are conducted, practices of visitors doing the walks, and when information from visits will be recorded are important. These processes and protocols must be transparent to all stakeholders impacted by classroom walkthroughs.

As you reflect on your role as instructional leader in your school, consider the following:

- How frequently do you plan to conduct classroom walkthroughs?
- Will you announce walkthroughs ahead of time?
- What are some guidelines you would expect of yourself and others in the conduct of walkthroughs? How will your staff inform your thinking?
- How will you track walkthroughs?

In Chapter Seven, we will explore more definitively the *focus* of various walkthrough observations. You will learn more about what specific practices and events to *look for* when walking in and out of classrooms.

7

Data Gathered During Classroom Walkthroughs

Walkthroughs provide important information about teacher behavior, student behavior, and overall classroom and school climate. We have covered different *purposes* for conducting walkthroughs, and in this chapter we will look at how the areas of *focus* and related *look-fors* for observations vary in relation to stated purposes. The focus of a walkthrough targets the general areas for collecting evidence of teaching and learning. Many focus questions that guide walkthroughs are an attempt to gather school-wide data to measure progress on a particular school or district improvement goal. Examples of focus questions are:

- What evidence demonstrates that students are actively engaged in their learning?
- How are diverse learning styles and multiple intelligences being accommodated?
- How is the use of higher-order thinking being demonstrated in lessons taught?
- How much and what type of writing are students doing across the curriculum?
- How are lessons being aligned to the state and district curriculum standards?

- How are teachers integrating technology into lessons to support student learning?
- What evidence illustrates that teachers are using formative assessments throughout lessons to monitor and adjust instruction?
- What developmentally appropriate activities are taking place to meet student needs?

Moving from a Focus Question to Look-Fors

A focus question can be further narrowed into "look-fors," or explicit teacher or student behaviors that participants will observe and record throughout their walks. Look-fors are clear statements or descriptors of observable evidence of teaching and learning such as specific instructional strategies, learning activities, behavioral outcomes, artifacts, routines, or practices. They are quantitative data that may assess both the degree of program implementation and needs of individual teachers, groups of teachers, the entire school, or school district. Broad focus areas as well as their related look-fors can be generated from such sources as the district strategic plan, school board goals, district benchmarks, curriculum standards, external regulatory mandates, the school improvement plan, professional development initiatives, and/or student achievement results. Focal points for observation can also be generated by individual teachers; grade, or subject-level, or department groups; or the entire faculty. Regardless of the focus, it is essential that teachers know what observers will be looking for in their walks.

Figure 7.1 shows two examples of a focus question and associated look-fors.

Figure 7.1:
Examples of Focus Questions and Associated Look-Fors

Focus Question:
How widely and effectively is guided reading being used to help students learn strategies for processing text with understanding?

Look-fors:
The teacher

- selects appropriately leveled reading materials for the group;
- assesses students' prior knowledge about the selection's topic and vocabulary;
- clarifies the purpose for reading a particular selection through prediction making, vocabulary introduction, or discussing ideas that

provide readers background knowledge required for understanding the text;

- observes students as they read the text softly or silently to themselves;
- provides guidance and coaching to students by providing prompts, asking questions, and encouraging attempts at the reading strategy application;
- asks questions to ensure text has been comprehended by readers;
- praises students' efforts in reading text;
- addresses second-language learners' needs.

Focus Question:
What evidence demonstrates that the amount of student writing across the curriculum is increasing?

Look-fors:
- students are able to explain the writing process;
- students are maintaining writing journals;
- examples of student writing are posted in the classroom;
- exemplar writing samples are posted in the classroom;
- prompts for journal writing are posted in the classroom;
- lesson plans include writing assignments;
- students share drafts of writing with each other.

In the above examples, each focus question and its accompanying look-fors must be discussed and understood by participants to assure that the data collected is based on consistent evidence useful for future planning.

Models Based on Research as a Foundation

As indicated in Chapter Three, some walkthrough models are based on a foundation of research on instructional practices that positively impact student learning (Figure 7.2). Most of the look-fors are clear statements or specific descriptors of observable evidence of this research base of teaching and learning strategies, activities, routines or practices.

The *Learning Walk® routine* is an organized visit through a school's halls and classrooms using the Principles of Learning as the lens to focus on the instructional core. These nine principles are condensed theoretical statements summarizing decades of learning research: (1) organizing for effort; (2) clear expectations; (3) fair and credible evaluations; (4) recognition of accomplishment; (5) academic rigor in a thinking curriculum; (6) Accountable Talk®; (7) socializing intelligence; (8) self-management of learning; and (9) learning as apprenticeship (Principles of Learning, 2007). The features of each principle are elaborated by a series of indicators that schools and classrooms are functioning in accordance with the given principle. Participants look for evidence of content-specific teaching and learning within the focus of the walk. They observe artifacts in the room such as wall charts and student portfolios. They listen to talk between teacher and students or students and students. When no direct whole-class instruction is occurring, walkers talk with students about their learning. This protocol is designed to help educators analyze the elements of instruction and opportunities for learning they offer to students.

> **Helpful Idea:** Connect your focus questions or look-fors to your state curriculum standards or professional development efforts so there is a common language understood by all.

The *(McREL) Power Walkthrough®* includes all classroom teachers and students in the school to determine the focus and look-fors. Using McREL research for professional development, participants gain a thorough understanding of the nine categories of instructional strategies in *Classroom Instruction that Works* (Marzano, Pickering, & Pollock, 2001) and are trained in how to identify these strategies in the classroom. Strategies include (1) identifying similarities and differences; (2) summarizing and note-taking; (3) reinforcing effort and providing recognition; (4) homework and practice; (5) nonlinguistic representations; (6) cooperative learning; (7) setting objectives and providing feedback; (8) generating and testing hypotheses; and (9) questions, cues, and advance organizers. Participants also observe how teachers and students integrate the use of technology into the lessons.

> **Helpful Idea:** A Protocol Bank of Professional Practice Indicators or look-fors is available for persons conducting walkthroughs from the Connecticut State Department of Education. (Connecticut Walkthrough Protocol Guide, 2008)

The *Teachscape Classroom Walkthrough (CWT)* protocol is designed for the collection and analysis of evidence on research-based practices proven effective in improving student achievement. Participants quickly collect data about critical instructional practices taking place across the school such as the use of questioning in the classroom (Bloom's Taxonomy); student engagement (Schlechty, 2001); use of the nine categories of effective instructional strategies (Marzano, Pickering, & Pollock, 2001); and degree of differentiation (Tomlinson, 1999). The focal points used for the walkthroughs are the elements of each of those research-based instructional practices. There is also a new version of CWT that is totally customizable by the users so that they can determine the research-based practices they wish to promote and observe.

Figure 7.2:
Look-fors in Walkthrough Models—Research as a Foundation

Models Based on Research as a Foundation	Look-fors
The Learning Walk® Routine	Are one or more of the Institute's Nine Principles of Learning and is content-specific and generated from the professional development offered.
(McREL) Power Walkthrough®	Relate to the nine strategies of *Classroom Instruction that Works* and teachers' and students' use of technology
Teachscape Classroom Walkthrough (CWT)	Include elements of research-based practices in use of questioning, student engagement, categories of effective instructional strategies, and degree of differentiation.

Models That Focus on Instructional and Curricular Practices

Several walkthrough models provide a protocol that meets a school's or district's intent to examine its own progress toward an initiative (Figure 7.3). That initiative can be related to curriculum, instruction, assessment, professional development, classroom organization and management, or a combination of school practices.

Martin Semmel, Principal, Bristol Central High School, Bristol, Connecticut, has led the development of the *Bristol Central High School Walk-Through*. This model contains a number of components similar to the

Teachscape Classroom Walkthrough (CWT) model but was modified to connect more explicitly to school and district goals. The Bristol walkthrough presents a transparent protocol for teachers and participants, embeds training for participants on specific look-fors, and collects valuable department- and school-level data. Data teams in each department developed focus questions and related look-fors to help teams concentrate on specific aspects of the education program. These focus questions and related look-fors are directly connected to the school improvement plan and the curriculum. In this way, the walkthrough protocol is seen as an integral part of the school improvement process.

The *Data-in-a-Day (DIAD)* protocol focuses on themes identified by the school that relate to the school's improvement plan and its professional development activities. Areas of the school such as the learning center, library, computer lab, gym, hallways, cafeteria, playground, and band room are all appropriate sites for data collection. The focus can be as diverse as school safety or how the faculty teaches problem solving. Observing research teams look for evidence that promotes or hinders actual learning. Some DIAD areas of focus ask:

1. Are students using a specific learning strategy?
2. Are students engaged inside the classrooms?
3. Is learning occurring at a deep level, beyond simply "covering the topic"?
4. Is the school an inviting place?
5. Are students well-behaved and respectful of teachers and one another?
6. Is the school providing enough support to English language learners?
7. Is the new program or school improvement initiative accomplishing the goals the school established?

The *Downey Three-Minute Classroom Walk-Through (CWT) with Reflective Practice* specifies five areas within which to focus observations (Downey et.al., 2004, pp. 20–42):

1. **Student orientation to work:** What are the students doing? Are they engaged or distracted? Behaving, or misbehaving?
2. **Curricular decisions:** What are the instructional objectives the teacher has chosen to teach? What is being taught? How aligned are the lesson objectives with the district goals and state standards/curriculum? What are the situations under which the students will demonstrate learning? What is the cognitive level of students' learning being demonstrated?

3. **Instructional strategies:** Does the teacher use a variety of strategies, such as hands-on work and small-group discussions to keep students engaged and interested? Does the teacher differentiate instruction to meet differing student learning styles and needs? Is the teacher asking higher-order questions?

4. **Walk the walls:** The observer notes what appears on the walls, bulletin boards, even ceilings in the classroom. What evidence is there of past objectives taught and/or instructional decisions used to teach the objectives that are present in the classroom?

5. **Health and safety conditions in the classroom:** The observer might notice the room temperature, lighting, science experiments being done without proper equipment, or uneven carpet or power cords that could represent hazards.

Twenty-Fourth Street Elementary School in Los Angeles, California, kicked off their inaugural classroom walkthrough with the entire school doing the walking. They elected to implement the process after school when the students were not present. A number of teachers volunteered and opened their classrooms to their peers. The visiting teachers chose a focus question and, in small groups, visited groups of classrooms, kindergarten through fifth grade. One example was a walkthrough to look for ideas on classroom environments that promoted literacy. In some situations, teachers took digital photographs as they toured classrooms so they could use the pictures as resources in designing their own room environments and instructional practices.

(Blatt, Linsley, & Smith, 2005)

Pete Hall, in his use of the *Hall Walk-Through*, focuses on the behaviors of teachers and students in the walkthroughs he plans. Hall arranges a preobservation conversation with the teacher to be observed in which they discuss expectations for the walk. This process enables differentiated look-fors based on the skills, experience, and needs of individual teachers. Look-fors can also come from a grade-level team's goal, especially if the goal lends itself to a particular instructional strategy. Sometimes the entire school staff will agree on certain look-fors because they align to elements of the schoolwide improvement plan (Hall & Simeral, 2008, pp. 131–132).

In the *High School Walkthrough* model the administrative team works together to identify look-fors based on the staff development teachers have experienced. In one particular case, the administrative team wanted data about how material was being presented in visual, auditory, and kinesthetic modes and the ways students were demonstrating their learning through those modes. The administrative team working with the staff identified specific data points related to the type of lesson presentation for participants to focus on during their walks (ASCD, 2007).

Deborah Tyler examines the instructional interaction between teachers and students through her *Instructional Walkthrough* model. She looks at:

- what the teacher is doing with the students (teacher talk, questioning);
- which key instructional and curricular initiatives are in place;
- the use of appropriate materials for teaching;
- what students are doing, their ability to explain what they are learning;
- student work displayed on the walls;
- types of assessment the classroom teacher is using to monitor learning.

The specific focus of the *Learning Keys' Data Walks* model is student engagement and involvement in the learning process. The model not only focuses on the teacher activities, but also uses the Schlechty (2001) model of measuring student engagement to provide a snapshot of student engagement in the learning process. For example, look-fors in a highly engaged classroom would include evidence that the majority of students are authentically engaged most of the time and all students are authentically engaged some of the time.

Characteristic of the *UCLA SMP Classroom Walk-Through* is that teachers are involved in the development of the focus question so they will have a personal stake in improvement efforts. Participants gather evidence of student learning based on pre-identified school-wide instructional or curricular initiatives, assessment efforts, or professional development learning. Assume that a school is working on increasing student engagement as a building-wide initiative. An example of a focus question might be, "What evidence do we see that students are actively engaged in their own learning?" The focus question serves as a guide for observers and evidence to be collected about how and what students are learning.

Helpful Idea: For maximum improvement potential, look at data gathered from walkthroughs with a school-wide focus rather than just an individual classroom focus.

The *Walkthrough Observation Tool* creates an intense focus on specific practices that improve students' learning and achievement. Look-fors for this model often reflect the district's standards for curriculum and instruction. This is important because the staff then has a common understanding of the indicators surrounding instruction and learning. Sources of data for look-fors include teacher behavior, materials utilized in instruction, physical arrangement of the classroom, class learning activities, student behavior and the level of student engagement. Talking to students about what they are doing and how they evaluate their work is another part of this model.

Figure 7.3:
Look-fors in Walkthrough Models—
Instructional and Curricular Practices

Models Focusing on Instructional and Curricular Practices	Look-fors
Bristol Central High School Walk-Through	Are dependent on the groups or individuals doing the walk. Usually the focus is lesson objectives, learning environment, level of student engagement, choice of instructional activities, or student work.
Data-in-a-Day (DIAD)	Are based on the themes identified by the school that are typically related to the school improvement plan or its professional development activities.
Downey Three-Minute Classroom Walk-Through (CWT) with Reflective Practice	Focus on five areas for observation: (1) student orientation to work; (2) curricular decisions; (3) instructional strategies; (4) walk the walls; and (5) health and safety conditions in the classroom.
Hall Walk-Through	Stem from pre-observation conversations between the administrator and the teacher or teachers related to their own goals, to grade-level team's goals, or to entire school staff's goals.
High School Walkthrough	Are based on the staff development teachers experienced. For example, the team may look at materials being presented in visual, auditory, and kinesthetic modes and how students demonstrated their learning.

Instructional Walkthrough	Are classroom instructional practices, curriculum, assessment, and learning environment and how these practices impact student achievement.
Learning Keys' Data Walks	Focus on learner objectives; rate at which objectives are being addressed; assessment methods being used; research-based instructional strategies used; level of student engagement; and richness of the learning environment.
UCLA SMP Classroom Walk-Through	Focus on collecting evidence of student learning impacted by instructional or curricular initiatives, assessment efforts, or professional development.
Walkthrough Observation Tool	Include students' behaviors, level of engagement, and quality of work. Focus is on noting student learning behaviors and products to determine which learning behaviors set the stage for success.

Models That Focus on Student Performance and Opportunities

Some walkthrough models focus on student performance and opportunities (Figure 7.5). How do they learn? Do they understand what they are learning? How do they feel about what they are learning? These questions illustrate examples of some of the look-fors that give observers a better picture of how effective instructional practices result in better performance.

The *Equity Learning Walk* examines the school's efforts to close the achievement gap and teach all students equitably. This protocol is designed as a *descriptive* visit where participants look for concrete evidence of equity in the school. Participants in equity learning walks notice specific practices to ensure high-quality education for all students: how equitable student participation is managed by the teacher; support for special education and ESL students; student seating arrangements that indicate equity; and evidence of high expectations for all students.

In the *Instructional Practices Inventory (IPI) Process*, observers collect data about student engagement in their own learning for the school's IPI profiles. The IPI provides formative data to guide collaborative faculty study and reflection. Decisions can then be made about how to effectively adjust instruction to increase student-engaged learning. The categories and look-fors in the IPI Process are found in Figure 7.4.

Figure 7.4:
Instructional Practices Inventory Categories (Form 6-07)*

Broad Categories	Coding Categories	Common Observer Look-fors
Student Engaged Instruction	Student-Active Engaged Learning	Students are engaged in higher-order learning. Common examples include authentic project work, cooperative learning, hands-on learning, problem-based learning, demonstrations, and research.
	Student Learning Conversations	Students are engaged in higher-order learning conversations. They are constructing knowledge or deeper understanding as a result of the conversations. Common examples are cooperative learning, work teams, discussion groups, and whole-class discussions. Conversations may be teacher stimulated but are not teacher dominated.
Teacher-Directed Instruction	Teacher-Led Instruction	Students are attentive to teacher-led learning experiences such as lecture, question and answer, teacher giving directions, and media instruction with teacher interaction. Discussion may occur, but instruction and ideas come primarily from the teacher. Higher-order learning is not evident.
	Student Work with Teacher Engaged	Students are doing seatwork, working on worksheets, book work, tests, video with teacher viewing the video with the students, etc. Teacher assistance, support, or attentiveness to the students is evident. Higher-order learning is not evident.
Disengagement	Student Work with Teacher not Engaged	Students are doing seatwork, working on worksheets, book work, tests, video without teacher support, etc. Teacher assistance, support, or attentiveness to the students is not evident. Higher-order learning is not evident.
	Complete Disengagement	Students are not engaged in learning directly related to the curriculum.

* Do not reproduce information from this chart without written permission from the developer.

Look 2 Learning (L2L) is another walkthrough model that has as its primary focus student *learning* rather than *teaching*. Each guiding question becomes a look-for and is written from the students' viewpoint. Using a simple recording format, principals, instructional coaches, team leaders, and/or classroom teachers make frequent classroom visits to collect information about student learning, student engagement, and student work. Look-fors include collecting data on the high-impact, leading indicators of learning, thus providing more focused information about learning. The L2L data analysis focus is a reflective group process that triangulates curriculum alignment, levels of thinking, quality of student work, learner engagement, and the instructional cycle. The L2L can also be customized to monitor school and district initiatives.

> **Milwaukee Public Schools** is an urban school district dedicated to creating and sustaining high performing classrooms that are organized to meet the learning needs of all students. The district is committed to providing a positive learning environment for students from diverse backgrounds in order to eliminate disparities in student achievement. Eight Characteristics of High Performing Urban Classrooms (CHPUC) and expectations for the schools and district support ensure that all classrooms are high performing and all students are achieving. Classroom walkthroughs are used to focus on the CHPUC *Active Engagement of Student Learners* and the evidence identified by local schools in their educational plan.
>
> Visit http://www2.milwaukee.k12.wi.us/supt/super/docs/EN/ brochure_urban.pdf

The observers of the **Mayerson Academy Classroom Walk-Through (CWT)** record evidence that students (1) learn rigorous content focused on achieving the standards; (2) are engaged in higher-level thinking and conversations about the concepts they are learning; (3) know what good work looks like and how they can make their work better; and (4) are aware of how they learn and have developed the habits and skills to assess their own learning.

In the **Palisades School District Walkthrough**, students talk about their work, describe the standards they used to create it, explain how their work is evaluated, and know how to improve it. This protocol requires teams of district and visiting educators to engage students in individual conversations about what they are learning. Two interviews are held each year, once in the fall and again in the spring. From the fall walkthrough, teachers analyze the interview data to determine which skills and understandings have been mastered and which areas require increased attention for the remainder of the year. The spring walkthroughs are used to gauge whether students have improved in the specific areas in which they had trouble in the fall. The content of the interviews is guided by a consistent set of questions that are compiled jointly by teachers and administrators and are tailored to the students' general educational level (primary, intermediate, middle, and high school).

Figure 7.5:
Look-fors in Walkthrough Models—
Student Performance and Opportunities

Models Focusing on Student Performance and Opportunities	Look-fors
Equity Learning Walk	Include attention to different learning styles, relationships between students and teachers, high expectations for all students, availability of resources to support different levels of language, and the use of differentiated instruction.
Instructional Practices Inventory (IPI) Process	Are quick-focus guides for the observer and are based on a coding process, grounded in six identified categories of student engagement.
Look 2 Learning (L2L) (formerly SMART Walks)	Are indicators of learning, analysis of curriculum alignment, levels of thinking and quality of student work, learner engagement, and the instructional cycle. The focus is on student *learning, engagement and work* rather than *teaching*.
Mayerson Academy Classroom Walk-Through (CWT)	Focus on questions used in observing and interviewing students that address rigorous content, higher-level thinking, student awareness of good work, and ability to assess their own learning.
Palisades School District Walkthrough	Focus on interviewing students in one-on-one conversations about their learning, their awareness of the standards used to create it, how their work is evaluated, and how to improve it.
School-Wide Walk-Through (James Hubert Blake High School)	Focus on student motivation whereby observers look at teaching strategies or decisions in action in classroom climate, relationships, literacy, and expectations.

At James Hubert Blake High School, every teacher participates in the *School-Wide Walk-Through,* and every teacher is visited. This staff is interested in student motivation, so they look for observable teaching strategies and teacher decisions that are likely to increase motivation. The major categories (high expectations, personal relationships, classroom climate, and literacy) and the related look-fors of this School-Wide Walk-Through are found in Figure 7.6.

Figure 7.6:
School-Wide Walk-Through Look-Fors

High Expectations	Personal Relationships
• Students make real world connections. • Students are independent thinkers and learners. • Teachers prepare students for the next stage of life. • Students are challenged to excel.	• Engagement or enjoyment is apparent. • Comfort, trust, and respect are evident. • There is teacher availability. • Teachers are motivating, inspiring, encouraging.
Classroom Climate	**Literacy**
• Teachers motivate as well as inspire. • Teachers are consistent and fair. • Teachers encourage students. • Students feel comfortable to take risks. • Students feel comfortable and safe (trust).	• Teachers model their own thinking strategies. • Students have "fix-up" strategies to help them through the text. • A buzz of excitement over literature can be heard. • Students ask thoughtful questions and give thoughtful answers. • Students are realistic about reading.

In Summary

Beyond establishing a well-defined purpose for conducting walk-throughs, specifying the focus or look-fors by those participants is extremely important. Look-fors describe observable evidence of teaching and learning such as instructional strategies, learning activities, behavioral outcomes, artifacts, routines, or practices. Sources of look-fors can relate to district or school improvement efforts and can be tailored to individual teachers or entire staffs.

As you reflect on your role as instructional leader in your school, consider the following:

- How will you collaborate with faculty to identify and refine the focus and look-fors that will lead to further professional development and improve instruction?

- What sources will you use for identifying a focus and look-fors for your walkthroughs?

- What look-fors do you consider important to note during classroom walkthroughs?

- What other data might you gather and analyze to complement evidence from walkthroughs?

In Chapter Eight, we will examine the options on how data from walkthrough observations are recorded for feedback. Examples of various feedback forms for recording data are introduced along with information on those software programs available for ease of information gathering, recording, and analysis.

8

Recording Data from Classroom Walkthroughs

A major consideration in your design of a walkthrough is how you will record the information you gather from the classroom visits. In this chapter, we will introduce you to formats that include checklists, narrative summaries, a combination of the two, and software programs available for simplifying the procedures for information gathering, recording, and analysis (Figure 8.7). The format most suited for you will depend on the purpose of your walkthrough, whether you will be looking for specific indicators of teacher or student behaviors, and the nature of feedback you intend to provide.

There are a number of other considerations, including:

- What are you going to record?
- How are you going to record observation data?
- How will you share this data with teachers and/or staff?
- Will you file this data in some record-keeping system?

Recording Forms

Like other walkthrough protocol decisions, it will be the purpose of the walkthrough that dictates what is best for recording observations. A checklist names very specific look-fors that can be easily observed. For walkthrough models aimed at verifying the compliance of specific elements of instructional, curricular, or other educational initiatives, checklists serve that purpose well. Checklists clarify for both the observer and observed the exact educational behaviors and activities expected. Checklists can provide a quick, easily recorded overview of day-to-day teaching and learning activities.

Some educators prefer not to use checklists for walkthroughs. Gary Bloom (2007) sees them as blunt instruments that produce superficial data and convey compliance-oriented supervision rather than collaboration with teachers (p. 42). Carolyn Downey says, "Checklists signal a formal observation and one that often looks like an inspection to the teacher" (2004, p. 4). Downey believes that walkthroughs should be about colleagues working together, helping each other think about teaching practices, not about judging a teacher's effective use of a specific teaching practice. She allows that some notation might be made to help recall a reflective question later when conversing with a teacher, but no copy of notes is given to the teacher and/or placed in a file. In fact, Merrill (2008) surveyed principals throughout Illinois and found that the use of informal notes was the predominate method of data collection during walkthroughs.

According to the Alberta (Canada) Teachers' Association (ATA), using a walkthrough process to place a check mark next to a descriptor on a list does little to improve instruction. ATA believes that working with teachers collaboratively, allowing professionals to share expertise with one another, is a more effective way to improve teaching practice and develop the capacity of the professionals in the school setting (Alberta Teachers' Association, 2006, p. 5).

Helpful Idea: Focus on just one or two very specific areas of teaching and learning during walkthroughs rather than trying to observe everything occurring in the classroom.

Narrative Forms

In the *School-Wide Walk-Through*, a capture sheet is used by each visiting team member. Team members write what they observe regarding teaching strategies or teachers' decisions in each of the categories: classroom climate, personal relationships, literacy support, and high expectations. Although this form is designed for narrative comments under each of the categories, specific look-fors that have been agreed upon prior to the visit are included on the form (Figure 8.1).

A narrative walkthrough observation form has been developed for the *Bristol Central High School Walk-Through* to capture data from each visit. Walking teams are allowed to use the whole form or a part of the form depending on the identified purpose for the walkthroughs. In addition, informational sheets were developed as supplements to the school-wide walkthrough form. These sheets help explain and identify what is meant by certain parts of the data collection form. For example, five levels/types of student engagement are identified on the walk-through form. The information sheets provide a definition for each type of engagement. These sheets allow the form to possess necessary white space for notes while keeping the educational vocabulary consistent.

The *UCLA SMP Classroom Walk-Through* protocol requires observations to be objective, not evaluative. The visiting team gathers data in response to the focus question, and they attend primarily to the evidence of student learning that relates to the focus. Team members note what students are doing, student work displayed, interactions between students and teacher, and interactions among students. They simply record their observations without interpretation and connect those observations with any notes, thoughts, and questions.

Helpful Idea: Align your classroom walkthrough with other school tools (school improvement plan, professional development initiatives, group analysis of student work, action research) aimed at improving student achievement.

Figure 8.1:
Narrative Observation Form with Look-Fors

Look-fors for Walk-Throughs – Period 1
Blake (Maryland) High School

As you visit a classroom, note the things you see in your category. Remember you should:
- write down exact quotes when possible instead of paraphrasing a teacher or student;
- refrain from talking about the classes you visit until the debriefing;
- use eye contact with the rest of your group to determine when it is time to leave each class; and
- talk quietly with a student if the lesson allows it—you can ask something about the category for which you are looking, or you can ask what happened in the lesson before you arrived, or something else relevant.

When you finish in your three classes, come back to the staff lounge to debrief.

High Expectations	Personal Relationships
• Students who make real world connections • Students who are independent thinkers and learners • Teachers who are preparing students for the next stage of life • Students who are challenged to excel.	• Engagement or enjoyment • Comfort, trust, respect • Availability • Motivating, inspiring, encouraging
Classroom Climate	**Literacy**
• Teachers who motivate as well as inspire • Teachers who are consistent and fair • Teachers who encourage students • A classroom where students are not afraid and where students feel comfortable to take risks • A classroom where students feel comfortable and safe (trust)	• Teachers who model their own thinking strategies as a way of aiding reading comprehension and understanding • Students who know when they do not understand text and apply "fix-up" strategies to help them through the text • A buzz of excitement over literature can be heard • Students ask thoughtful questions and give thoughtful answers • Students who are realistic about reading: "Reading is hard and hard is necessary"

The *Hall Walk-Through* Reflection Form is a narrative form that includes a targeted look-for, a clear outline of what the administrator hopes or expects to see based on a pre-observation discussion with the teacher(s). The observer records the day's look-for on one line. The remainder of the form includes the name of the teacher, date of visit, time of visit, content being observed, and narrative space for recording responses to "What is the TEACHER doing?", "What are STUDENTS doing?", and "Comments" (Figure 8.2).

The Learning Walk® routine participants use an open-ended form that lends itself to notes about any type of evidence observed but identifies neither specific room numbers nor teachers. These recording sheets are used by participants for note-taking and are not shared with others. Participants use the information collected privately to create a debrief document in which they identify trends and patterns observed across classrooms. A feedback letter from the principal or a faculty meeting is held to share patterns and questions identified by walkers and usually identifies follow-up professional development topics and information about the next learning walk.

In the *Palisades School District Walkthrough* model, teachers create questions for observers to ask students. Response sheets are used to record the students' answers that are documented in a manner that lends itself to both quantitative and qualitative analysis. At the Palisades Middle School, Principal Ed Baumgartner reported that the teachers created questions specially designed to solicit responses from the students concerning their perceptions of Daniel H. Pink's *Six Creative Senses* (Pink, 2006). A Student Perception Assessment Form is provided for each observer to record information on the questions created to be asked of students (Figure 8.3).

For the *Equity Learning Walk, Instructional Walkthrough, High School Walkthrough* and *Walkthrough Observation Tool* models, written narratives of observations are recorded on a notepad or an index card. The notes reflect observation data for later analysis and conversations as teachers receive feedback and reflect on the data.

The Hall Walk-Through Reflection Form

Teacher:_____ Date:_____ Time: _____

Content: _____

Look-for Focus _____

What is the TEACHER doing?

_____

_____

_____

_____

What are STUDENTS doing?

_____

_____

_____

_____

Comments:

_____

_____

_____

_____

_____

_____

_____

Student Name: _____

Building: PALMS

PALISADES MIDDLE SCHOOL WALKTHROUGH

STUDENT PERCEPTION ASSESSMENT

QUESTIONS:	NOTES:	YES	NO
Design • I am able to find solutions to problems without a lot of help. • I have created something new on my own.			
Story • I am able to communicate to others verbally and in writing.			
Symphony • I am able to identify strengths / weaknesses in my own work. • I am able to work with others in a group.			
Empathy • I am able see opposing points of view.			
Play • There are opportunities for learning to be fun in the classroom. • I am able to use creativity in my schoolwork.			
Meaning • I am able to identify, gather, and use information / data. • I am willing to take risks to solve a problem.			
One way in which my teachers help me be creative is….			
In what areas am I most creative?			

Checklist Forms

Ruby Payne provides checklist notepads that include rubrics to quantify progress in the classroom with the *Payne School Model* (http://www.ahaprocess.com/store/Materials.html). This model is designed to increase student achievement and develop capacity in teachers to more effectively meet the needs of their students. Payne offers five different walkthrough rubrics: general walkthroughs; walkthroughs for mutual respect; walkthroughs for instruction; walkthroughs for discipline and classroom management; and audits for differentiated instruction (see Figure 8.4 for a sample of the Payne Walkthrough for Instruction Rubric).

Figure 8.4:
Payne Walkthrough for Instruction Rubric

WALKTHROUGH FOR INSTRUCTION RUBRIC

Issue	Present	Needed	N/A
Students use mental models			
Procedures are used by students to work through lesson (e.g., step sheets)			
Lesson is tied to standard			
Checks for understanding used throughout lesson			
Guided practice opportunities provided for students			
Students have tools for self-evaluation of student work (rubric, checklists, etc.)			
Student work/assignments are calibrated to grade level			
Teachers use models during instruction			
Student work/assignments are differentiated			

Teacher name _____   Date _____

Signature _____

Material adapted from *A Framework for Understanding Poverty* www.ahaprocess.com
Copyright © 2004 aha! Process, Inc. All rights reserved.

In schools awarded a Reading First (Title 1B of No Child Left Behind) grant, personnel are assigned to conduct regular walkthroughs using grade-by-grade checklists (Figure 8.5). Because one of the requirements of continuous federal funding is assurance that instructional and curricular elements of the Reading First program are in place, classroom walkthrough checklists serve as guidelines to administrators of precisely what to observe.

For the *Instructional Practices Inventory (IPI) Process*, observational data is gathered through the lens of the six categories that distinguish among the types of learning experiences in which students are engaged. Although not exactly a checklist, the data coding form is designed to allow observers to record the existence and compile the frequency of student engagement per the six categories and combinations of the six categories (Figure 7.4). Two categories document higher order, deeper learning experiences among the majority of students in the classroom. Three categories are primarily teacher-directed, non-higher-order engagement focusing on simple understanding, recall, practice, and skill development. One category is student disengagement. Data is transferred by code number from the data coding form to a spreadsheet that portrays the observations organized into the six categories in pie chart format for core curriculum (math, science, social studies, and language arts), non-core curriculum, and all curricula. All data codes are anonymous, and data is compiled for the whole school.

Combination Forms

A combination of checklist and narrative helps in managing productive conversations about the visits in other situations. As an example, Robert Miller, principal of St. Charles East High School in St. Charles, Illinois, and his administrative team developed such a combined checklist/narrative form to use for their walkthroughs (Figure 8.6). The walkthrough form includes a checklist of the look-fors on the part of both teacher and student actions and the use of Bloom's Taxonomy, but it also allows the classroom visitor to record descriptive comments of observations.

Principal's Reading Walkthrough for Third Grade Reading First Classrooms

Teacher_____ Grade Level_____ Date_____

Classroom Environment
☐ Classroom is arranged to enable active engagement by all students.
☐ Daily Class Schedule is posted which includes a minimum of 90 minutes for reading instruction plus an additional block of time for intensive intervention.
☐ Program components are evident and in use indicating a print rich environment (e.g., decodable books, student readers, leveled texts, vocabulary words, letter-sound cards, etc.)

Materials
☐ Teacher and student materials are accessible and organized.
☐ Evidence exists of program materials being used as designed.

Teacher Instruction
☐ Classroom behavior management system is effective in providing an environment conducive to learning.
☐ Teacher follows the selected program's instructional routines as designed.
☐ Teacher uses explicit instruction and scaffolds instruction.
☐ Teacher fosters active student engagement and motivation to learn.
☐ Pacing is appropriate and transitions are smooth and quick.

Whole Class Instruction
☐ Instruction is focused on the content of the lesson in the teacher's edition.
☐ Teacher uses a variety of resources during reading instruction (e.g., decodable books, vocabulary word lists, letter-sound cards, etc.).

Small-Group, Differentiated Instruction
☐ Small-group instruction is provided at different levels depending on student need.
☐ Differentiated, small-group instruction or time for direct work with individuals is a regular daily activity, as evidenced by the posted classroom schedule.

Student Reading Centers
☐ Centers are clearly defined and labeled.
☐ Students remain engaged during centers and independent work.

Phonics
☐ Visual aids (alphabet cards and letter/sound cards) are used as designed by program.
☐ Teacher provides explicit instruction of letter sounds and blending strategies.
☐ Students apply letter/sound knowledge in reading and writing activities.

The observation instruments for *Data-in-a-Day (DIAD)* are developed specifically for each school so that the language is familiar to the schools' students and parent/community members. The forms can be a combination of open-ended questions that result in narrative notes and a short checklist of specific actions that would be readily observed. The collection instruments must be easily understood by all members of the school community. Teams record objective notes of specific examples that illustrate key themes they observe in their walks. The faculty later uses the data gathered to determine the next steps.

Administrators in the **Brockton Public Schools, Brockton, Massachusetts**, developed a "School Visit Walkthrough Guide" and modified it based on feedback from walkthrough teams. The walkthrough guide was presented to and discussed extensively with principals who presented it to their teachers, all of whom are now familiar with the instrument. The walkthrough guide is used by a team of central curriculum administrators, led by the deputy superintendent, who schedule three–four walkthroughs per school per year. The walkthroughs have proven to be a very effective means of monitoring and changing classroom practice. The central administrative walkthrough team visits the Commonwealth Priority Schools (three schools that have very different sets of problems and issues from the other public schools) regularly and uses the same walkthrough guide to gather feedback about the visits.

Brockton Public Schools (2008)

Figure 8.6:
Checklist/Narrative Observation Form Sample

St. Charles (Illinois) East High School
Classroom Walkthrough Form

CLASSROOM DATA

Time of Observation:

Opening___ Middle ___ Closing ___

Time In: ____ Time Out: ___

Subject: _____ Period: _____ Class Size: _____

Classroom Observation	Description/ Comments	Department Specific
Teacher Actions		
☐ Agenda posted		
☐ Clear learning objectives		
☐ Evidence of planning for instruction		
☐ Teacher explains/demonstrates		
☐ Lecture		
☐ Choice for students (involving students in decisions that affect learning		
☐ Teacher modeling with student praise		
☐ Teacher-led instruction/ discussion		
☐ Teacher shows positive relationship with students		
☐ Teacher meets individual student's needs (differentia-tion)		
☐ Team Teaching—each teacher leads instruction		
☐ Effective questioning and discussion		
☐ Timely feedback given to students		
☐ Adequate wait time		
☐ Makes interdisciplinary connections		
☐ Uses technology		
☐ Addresses multiple intelli-gences		
☐ Classroom management		

Student Actions		BLOOM'S TAXONOMY
☐ Warm-up/closure activity ☐ Students show positive relationship with teacher ☐ Reading/Writing ☐ Applying previous knowledge ☐ Hands-on student work ☐ Active learning ☐ Cooperative learning – student groups/partners ☐ Using technology ☐ Students are participating ☐ Students demonstrate understanding ☐ Student presentations ☐ Worksheet/text seat work		☐ Knowledge ☐ Comprehension ☐ Application ☐ Analysis ☐ Synthesis ☐ Evaluation
OVERALL CLASSROOM ENVIRONMENT		COMMENTS
EVIDENCE OF LEARNING	☐ Low ☐ Medium ☐ High	
STUDENTS ON TASK ☐	STUDENTS OFF TASK ☐	

Figure 8.7:
Walkthrough Data Collection Processes

Models	Collection Processes
Bristol Central High School Walk-Through	A walkthrough observation form is used to capture data from each visit. Teams are allowed to develop their own data gathering forms.
Data-in-a-Day (DIAD)	Teams note specific examples of evidence that illustrate the key themes that are the focus of their walks. Observation instruments are developed specifically for each school using language students and parents can understand.
Downey Three-Minute Classroom Walk-Through (CWT) with Reflective Practice	There are no checklists for the observations. Observers may take notes for their own memory; however, no copy of notes is given to the teacher or placed in a file.
Equity Learning Walk	Observers record concrete examples of evidence revealing equity in the school.
Hall Walk-Through	Observers use the *Hall Walk-Through Reflection Form* for narrative recordings. The form includes Look-for focus & narrative space for recording responses to "What is the teacher doing?", "What are students doing?", and "Comments."
High School Walkthrough	Observers record five different pieces of information they have collected in each classroom that show evidence of a new initiative within the school.
Instructional Practices Inventory (IPI) Process	Data is gathered through the lens of the six Instructional Practices Inventory (IPI) categories. For each category, there is a distinct way of codifying how the majority of the students in the learning setting are engaged.
Instructional Walkthrough	Observers write notes on a form attached to a clipboard. Content of form includes look-fors identified by teachers.
Learning Keys' Data Walks	Observations are recorded on a PDA or Blackberry. Data can be uploaded to the desktop computer and then to the building/district data system to electronically create reports sorted and separated by building, district, and date.

The Learning Walk® Routine	Participants use an open-ended form that lends itself to notes about any type of evidence. The form identifies neither specific room numbers nor teachers.
Look 2 Learning (L2L) (formerly SMART Walks)	Using a simple recording format, observers record information about student learning, student engagement, and student work. Information can also be recorded electronically using L2L software on a PDA, smart phone, or desktop computer.
Mayerson Academy Classroom Walk-Through (CWT)	Observers use a CWT Building Summary form that has notes of what they saw/heard and recommendations for improvement. The form includes indicators for the use of Bloom's Taxonomy and a student interview form.
(McREL) Power Walk-through®	Observations are recorded on a PDA, Tablet PC, IPhone, Blackberry, or device loaded with McREL's Web-based software. Data is transmitted to the Internet to build reports/graphs of the school's instructional activity to determine the extent to which professional development is evident in the classrooms.
Palisades School District Walkthrough	Observers record student responses to 7–9 specific questions. Student responses are documented and summarized for both a quantitative and qualitative analysis.
School-Wide Walk-Through	A capture sheet is used. Each team member writes what he/she observed regarding teaching strategies or decisions related to classroom climate, relationships, literacy, or expectations.
Teachscape Classroom Walkthrough (CWT)	Data is collected using the Teachscape research-based tool and data-collection software on a handheld device. Data is then transmitted to the Internet to build a picture (reports, graphs) of the school's instructional activity.
UCLA SMP Classroom Walk-Through	Observers record their observations without interpretation and connect those observations with any notes, thoughts, and questions. There are no checklists.
Walkthrough Observation Tool	Observers write notes of specific examples of effective practice and exact details about the implementation/use of look-fors.

Software Tools for Walkthroughs

Recordkeeping of observations from multiple walkthroughs can be a real challenge. Furthermore, to summarize and analyze such information from many walks and prepare feedback either to specific teachers or groups of teachers adds to the complexity of the effort. In light of these challenges, technology has helped by simplifying the process extending from conducting walkthroughs to analyzing results for feedback. A number of organizations have developed walkthrough software that is compatible with handheld devices like personal digital assistants (PDAs) and mobile telephones for recording and storing data. While some software allows for the downloading of data to a desktop computer for later review and analysis, other software provides for the uploading of observational data to a website. Some software organizations offer customized options that allow schools to digitize their current walkthrough observation form to incorporate their own existing terminology, focus, descriptors, and/or initiatives. The use of technology in the walkthrough process is especially appropriate in districts where teachers and students are expected to use technology for teaching and learning.

Preferred Educational Software markets electronic software using a checklist format known as *The Administrator Observer*. Optimized for walkthroughs, it will also document longer visits. Generic standards-based templates, which are easily replaced with local standards and objectives, are provided. Observers use a handheld device to indicate and rate which standards were observed. The principal can upload the record of observations to a desktop to create a feedback in several formats. Output to PDF format allows prompt email feedback to the teacher. Frequency distributions and mean values provide data for school improvement and direction for staff development, and a variety of graphs can be generated easily. Handheld devices supported include Palm, Windows Mobile, Blackberry, and most smart phones. Go to www.theadministrativeobserver.com.

CWT Max, offered by Educator Software Solutions, allows administrators to record data they want to collect about their visits to classrooms and view reports based on this information. CWT runs on a PDA, desktop, or a Microsoft Tablet PC. The software can also be installed on PDA smart phones such as the Palm Treo. Go to http://www.educatorsoftwaresolutions.com/default.htm.

eCOVE Observation Software supports classroom walkthroughs, sit-downs, and in-depth classroom observations. The eCOVE Software is a large collection of objective data collection tools and can be formatted to meet specific data collection needs or to align with district or national standards. eCOVE has different versions of templates for school administrators, special education, and second language instruction. Reports can be generated for individuals or groups for a single observation, an individual or group over time, or a comparison of individuals or groups. The data can be printed with graphs or exported to Excel. eCOVE Observation Software supports Palm and Pocket PC handhelds, as well as Windows or Macintosh laptops. The website includes training videos and free overview webinars. Go to http://www.ecove.net.

Observer Classroom Observation Software is designed to assist administrators in recording walkthroughs. There is a desktop version on which administrators can do observation entries directly on the PC and a version for entries on a Palm with ability to sync observations to a PC. Observers can create and edit the observation items that the program uses. All data can be hosted on a PC or server, and observation results can be reported for individuals, by grade level, or by subject. Multiple observations can also be combined into one report. Go to http://www.papertrailsoftware.com/observer/index.html.

Springboard Schools has developed the SpringWare™ Suite of data tools that provides educators with the data analysis tools from which they can summarize patterns and trends for improvement efforts. SpringWare tools include **SpringWare™ WT,** a principal's classroom walkthrough tool that helps collect consistent data, aggregates for one or many schools, and creates data-based reports. Each data tool comes with help for installation on a personal system or a district network. Go to http://www.springboardschools.org/tools_resources/springware.html.

A number of educational technology companies have developed walkthrough programs that utilize very specific research-based information to guide observations and be recorded on handheld devices. For example, the **iObservation™ system** developed by Learning Sciences International is a data collection tool for conducting short, frequent, formative classroom walkthroughs. Based on the research of national experts, iObservation system forms provide clarity using explicit terminology, descriptions, and examples of effective teaching practices. Each observation form is featured by a video that models effective instructional strategies; look-fors that define effective classroom instructional behaviors; rubrics that explain each level on the growth continuum; coaching tips that guide administrators to provide feedback appropriately scaffolded to teachers' progress along the growth continuum; evidence collection that allows artifacts such as lesson plans and student work samples to be filed electronically; and a comments section for feedback that is built directly into the form for convenience. Go to http://www.iobservation.com/iobservation/solutions.cfm.

Teacher Evaluation and Student Data Classroom Walk-Through software produced by Austin Sky Technology can be customized to meet a school's classroom walkthrough requirements and emulate a school's rubric on a handheld device. This software allows walkthrough participants to record any kind of observations with a Windows Mobile/Pocket PC handheld computer, laptop, desktop or Tablet PC. The software is adaptable for many styles of walkthroughs, such as three-minute walkthroughs, third-party walkthroughs, narrative or quantitative styles, or Danielson/McGreal-type approaches. Go to http://www.austinsky.com/classroomwalkthrough.html.

Other organizations have developed software for recording on very specific research-based observation data on hand-held devices that can also be uploaded to the Internet for analysis and summary and downloaded in building-wide or district-wide reports.

LoTi Connection, Inc. provides an online tool called the *LoTi Observer* that automatically calculates a teacher's LoTi Level based on an administrator's recorded walkthrough observations using an iPod Touch. This walkthrough model is known as H.E.A.T (Higher order thinking, Engaged learning, Authenticity, and Technology use) and is intended to improve instruction and student achievement. H.E.A.T. walkthroughs can be customized to reflect specific district initiatives (e.g., Daggett's Rigor & Relevance, Marzano's Research-based Best Practices, Wiggins and McTighe's Understanding by Design, Big 6 Research Model) and any other classroom look-fors. Go to http://www.loticonnection.com/heatwalkthroughs.html.

(McREL) Power Walkthrough® Classroom Observation Software enables the observer to conduct and record informal observations in individual classrooms. The software helps school leaders record data on handheld devices such as a PDA, Tablet PC, Blackberry, or iPhone loaded with McREL's web-based software. The software helps the observer focus on factors that research shows to influence student learning such as effective instructional strategies, student engagement, and teachers' use of technology. While the Power Walkthrough® process conducts and records informal observations in individual classrooms, the emphasis is on aggregating the data to the building and district level. Power Walkthrough® software makes it easy to upload observation data to the Internet and to the computer to generate customized reports for individuals or groups of teachers, entire schools, and even districts. Charts and graphs of observable data can be generated. Go to http://www.mcrel.org/powerwalkthrough.

Software for the *Learning Keys' Data Walks* can be downloaded from the website and then synchronized onto the handheld device. The device is then used to record data during walkthroughs. Information is coordinated via a computer, and data for the site is compiled. Templates have been developed for aligning walkthrough data to the components of the Data Walks. These templates can then be customized for additional features as desired by individual districts. Go to http://www.learningkeys.org/KeyPlays/DataWalksPDA/tabid/170/Default.aspx.

Look 2 Learning (L2L) has a software option that provides an electronic collection of information that store to a web-based analysis program. The results are displayed graphically, yet allow for narrative and anecdotal records. The information can be cross-tabulated to triangulate rigor, relevance, and curricular alignment. The ability to compare data across time periods allows schools to understand and target student learning issues and monitor action plans for improvement. The L2L software fully integrates with lesson-design software (Lessons 4 Learning) that allows teachers to design student learning based upon the high-impact leading indicators that are the look-fors of L2L. These lesson plans can be stored and shared at the teacher's discretion. Further, the lessons can serve as a curriculum or instruction map for the school. Go to http://www.colleaguesoncall.com.

SRI International and the Miami Museum of Science worked together to develop **PD3, Professional Development Decisions Using Data**, a walkthrough tool specifically for principals to identify the professional development needs of teachers in the areas of mathematics and science. The PD3 reading component was developed by Miami-Dade County Public Schools, the Florida Center for Reading Research, SRI, and the Museum. PD3 consists of a classroom visit data collection tool on a handheld computer and a website that enables users to generate online reports based on aggregated observation data. PD3 Online Reports use the data collected about the instruction and content of the lesson to guide a school's or district's professional development for teachers within grade levels or subject areas. Go to http://pd3.miamisci.org/index.php.

Teachscape Classroom Walkthrough (CWT) Technology is a simple data collection application that can be added to most wireless handheld devices. Research-based tools and data collection software on a handheld device enable instructional leaders to quickly collect data about critical instructional practices. Once uploaded, this data is shaped into reports and graphs. Teachers can access Teachscape's online resource library, which includes "learning modules" that outline effective ways to improve teaching. Go to http://www.teachscape.com/html/ts/nps/classroom_walkthrough.html.

ThinkData, developed by The Management Solution, Inc., is a system designed to help schools and districts regularly look at large numbers of classes in a short period of time. This is a web-based technology that can be used as easily with a smart phone as it can with a pencil and paper. ThinkData allows the classroom visitor to look at items that are of interest and provides results quickly enough to meet with other educators the same day to discuss the data. Observation data can be tracked over time and used to measure the effectiveness of the professional development programs and promote relevant discussions about instruction in the schools. Go to http://www.TheManagementSolution.com.

For a number of these observation software organizations, on-site hands-on training and technical support in the use of the software are available. Most of these organizations customize the training and use of software to support district or state standards.

Principals who have used handheld devices for collecting observation data have shared a number of recommendations. First, determine the purpose and protocol for the kind of walkthrough you want in your schools. Then, research the various models and determine which software and handheld device will be most appropriate and manageable. Third, pilot the new device and software prior to making any large-scale purchases. Fourth, seek input from your teachers on their views and understanding of the value of such technology. And last, make sure that training and on-going technical assistance are provided in the use of the software used on handheld devices.

In Summary

Individuals conducting walkthroughs can record their observations in a wide variety of ways. Those include narrative forms, forms with checklists only, and forms with checklists and narrative space combined. Some have structured forms, and others are simply note paper for observation notes. Some of the forms will be given back to teachers, and they may be used to recall observations for follow-up conversations. Other notes will be collected and aggregated across multiple teacher observations to create a school-wide or district-wide profile of practices. Some observers will mark on checklists or write narrative comments in the classroom while others will wait until they leave the classroom and make notes immediately after the walk. Technology is available to assist with recording data as well as generating a variety of reports from the data.

As you reflect on your role as instructional leader in your school, consider the following:

- Will it be necessary to collect observational data from all of your walkthroughs?
- Will you write notes as you observe or wait until the observation is completed?

- How will you organize your notations from walkthroughs to give feedback?
- Will technology be helpful for your classroom walkthrough data collection?

As Maureen Nichols, Instructional Data Specialist, School District of Philadelphia, Pennsylvania, sums it up, "No matter what form is used, the ultimate goal is to support school communities as they strive to implement their school improvement plans and assist professionals to create the conditions that will optimize the learning environment for all stakeholders" (M. Nichols, personal communication, June 22, 2009).

The focus in Chapter Nine will be on the follow-up to walkthroughs given to individual teachers, groups of teachers, or the entire school.

9

Providing Follow-up on Classroom Walkthroughs

If walkthroughs are going to improve teaching and learning, follow-up to teachers is essential. Follow-up can be given in written or oral form and can be formal or informal (Figure 9.1). Brief notes placed in the teachers' mailboxes or sent by e-mail are common ways of follow-up and usually include a summary of key observations, comments, points for clarification, and possible ideas for the teacher. Although follow-up can be given informally between classes or in a casual visit before or after school, it is more common to schedule a specific time to discuss or reflect on the observation. This also provides the opportunity to learn more about what took place before and after the classroom visit that may enhance the observer's understanding.

You will notice the theme of "reflection" throughout this chapter. Walkthroughs are used to facilitate conversations about teaching and learning, so it is helpful to encourage teachers to reflect on their teaching practices relative to student achievement.

Follow-up with Individual Teachers

The hoped-for outcome of walkthroughs is that teachers closely examine their practices and become increasingly reflective, self-directed, critical thinkers focused on continually improving their teaching. The reflective conversations following walkthroughs provide teachers with another perspective on their instruction. Killion and Todnem (1991, p. 15) mention "reflection-*on*-action" as a frequent image educators have when they first think about reflection. It is the *looking back* at actions or decisions and musing about why one thought a certain way or made certain decisions. However, it is "reflection-*for*-action" those authors convey as having the greatest value for teachers in feedback conversations. "Reflection-*for*-action" guides teachers in the future decisions and actions they plan to take to improve their instruction and impact student performance.

According to Hall and Hord (2000, p. 111), the brief, one-on-one conversation about what was observed or heard is the most powerful staff development approach available to impact teacher behavior. The goal of such dialogue is to use questions that encourage teachers to reflect on their classroom practice. When the educators in the school openly discuss what matters in the classroom, the possibilities for continuous improvement increase rather significantly.

Charlotte Danielson (2009, p. 103) believes that on-going, informal dialogue between school leaders and teachers is the foundation for improved classroom instruction, increased learner achievement, and more substantive discussions about education. She underscores the critical function of informal reflective professional conversations in continual teacher learning. Such conversations are extremely important in promoting a positive environment of inquiry, support, and teacher professional development. Danielson believes school leaders need to develop the communication skills to initiate and engage in successful conversations with teachers.

The goal of the ***Downey Three-Minute Classroom Walk-Through (CWT) with Reflective Practice*** is to create powerful learning that moves teachers to self-reflection, self-analysis, and self-direction to change or improve the choices they make as they teach (2004, p. 14). In subsequent writings, Downey and her colleagues (2009) have moved away from using the word "feedback" altogether. She explains that the word "feedback" means that one person tells another individual what one thinks about the other's work. This is evaluative and seldom leads to long-term sustained growth. She believes that follow-up dialogue is the approach to use—one in which motivating, meaningful conversations take place and the individual reflects on his or her work.

The premise of the ***Bristol Central High School Walk-Through*** is that one of the most powerful outcomes of the process is the discussion that occurs afterward. The observation team decides on the kind of follow-up that will be provided to the teacher. Typically, a non-judgmental, reflective question is added to encourage thought on a specific area of the teaching and learning process. Although e-mail is sometimes used, a face-to-face conversation is preferable because it encourages dialogue and further reflection. The administrative team also includes examples of excellent teaching observed during walkthroughs in its weekly e-bulletin to staff. The administrative team believes that this practice not only lowers the anxiety of staff members about the walkthrough process but also increases the level of reflection of all teachers as they consider the instructional strategies highlighted in the e-bulletin.

The **Spokane School District** has implemented a walkthrough protocol in which staff from the central office and building administrators jointly conduct walkthroughs to look for "three Cs and an E" — Curriculum content being taught, level of expected Cognitive ability according to Bloom's Taxonomy, classroom and lesson Context, and evidence of student Engagement. Teachers receive follow-up in the form of the walkthrough committee's shared perceptions and questions designed to encourage the teachers to think deeply about their teaching strategies and curriculum. Principals share their observations with the teachers as well, often providing reflective questions to prompt a continuing dialogue about teaching practices. The purpose of these walkthroughs is to provide a snapshot of a group of classrooms that will inform supervisors of the demands and challenges in their schools (Sather, 2004).

In the *Hall Walk-Through* model, the supervisor writes brief, specific comments on the *Hall Walk-Through Reflection Form* (Figure 8.2) and leaves a copy on the teacher's desk on the way out. The follow-up discussion with the teacher focuses on a critical analysis of the teacher's instructional practices, decision making, and thinking processes (Hall & Simeral, 2008, p. 137). The supervisor's goal is to guide each individual teacher along the *Continuum of Self-Reflection*, a tool to help school leaders understand a teacher's current state of mind and identify the approaches that will encourage deeper reflective habits (pp. 40–44).

Helpful Idea: Use the walkthrough as a tool for creating a collaborative learning community of professionals who continuously reflect about ways to improve teaching and learning.

In the *Mayerson Academy Classroom Walk-Through (CWT)*, the principal follows up with the teacher to discuss what was observed and then asks questions to provoke deep thinking about ways to advance student learning. When there is a team of observers, the participants assemble to give the teacher an overview and specific comments about what they observed. The team will identify trends, areas of strength, and a reflective question for the teacher. All of these are designed to encourage thoughtful dialogue and more critical thinking about lessons, curriculum, and teaching strategies.

Group Follow-up

Many walkthrough models are designed to collect information on the progress of a particular program or initiative. Follow-up is provided to a group or whole faculty for their reflection and discussion and opportunity to plan improvement. David Cohen, principal of Midwood High School in Brooklyn, New York, initiated a periodic newsletter (see Appendix D: Learning Walk Newsletter) to his faculty as a follow-up to teacher teams visiting classrooms for what he refers to as "learning walks." Cohen included information on the mission of the learning walk teams and examples of what they noted during their walks. Cohen found the newsletter to be a powerful means to overcome initial faculty anxiety and concern about the walks. The newsletter also promoted ongoing dialogue about instructional methodologies and gave teachers the opportunity to share teaching strategies.

As part of the *School-Wide Walk-Through*, every teacher in the school is visited, and every teacher serves on a visiting team to observe, discuss, and analyze teaching and learning. When visiting teams return to a meeting room, they discuss their observations and findings. A voluntary debriefing session is held at the end of the day involving the visiting teams and teachers observed. Findings are confidential and are not discussed beyond the agreed-upon audience. There are five ground-rules in the voluntary debrief session with teachers:

1. Consider what the data does and doesn't tell us;
2. Listen to hear first, and then respond;
3. Support broad generalizations with specific examples;
4. Refrain from using teachers' names or subjects taught when referring to observations; and

5. Consider the implications these trends and patterns have on one's teaching.

Classroom teachers are also the participants of the **UCLA SMP Classroom Walk-Through** both as observers and as classroom hosts. Observation data is compiled and shared when the teams come together for a debriefing session. Observers sit in a circle or semi-circle while teachers who were visited watch and listen to their discussion. In round-robin style, observers use this first phase of the debriefing to share and review charted observations related to the focus question. This allows everyone to view the information. They proceed through reflective conversation to identify patterns or themes within and across classrooms and to raise questions for further professional learning and investigation suggested by the patterns. The ultimate goal is to arrive at recommendations that further improve classroom practice to increase student understanding.

Helpful Idea: Share the positives of what you observe on your walk-throughs with all of the staff highlighting ideas others might find valuable.

Robin Wiltison, principal of Martin Luther King, Jr. Middle School in Beltsville, Maryland, sends a quarterly letter (see Appendix E: Walkthrough Feedback Letter) to her faculty, including the focus for that month's walks, a summary of observations, and a section entitled "Wonderings" to provoke conversations about teaching and learning. These learning walk teams involved King Middle School teachers as well as Hyattsville Middle School teachers in the same district.

One traditional method for follow-up for *The Learning Walk® routine* includes a letter sent by the principal to the entire school community. The faculty receives a compilation of patterns and questions identified by walkers that leads to potential professional development topics. Information regarding the next learning walks are often included as part of the follow-up process.

In the **Data-in-a-Day (DIAD)** model, observing team members assemble into small analysis groups to share and interpret their walkthrough observations around a self-study focus area given to them by the school. The staff is then provided a "snapshot" of the school in relation to the self-study area. The process promotes reflection and discussion about what is important at

At first I felt classroom walkthroughs were going to be awkward for the students, myself, and the administrator. Later, I learned that walkthroughs were a great opportunity to show off some of the wonderful learning we do everyday once our classroom door closes and it's typically just the kids and myself. I enjoy hearing my students explain what they're learning to the administrator. I also appreciate that the walkthroughs keep me on my toes to be sure that my classroom is set up properly for optimal learning and that instructional time is used wisely.

Shantelle Rieves, Third Grade Teacher,
Sawgrass Bay Elementary School Clermont, FL

the school while it encourages both students and staff to highlight themes that are areas of concern for both groups.

Equity Learning Walk teams gather to discuss what they learned from the process and offer "warm and cool" follow-up to the school's leadership team on such areas as attention to different learning styles, high expectations for all students, and the use of differentiated instruction. They engage the school's leadership team in dialogue about the evidence of equity observed and where opportunities for increased equity could occur. The leadership team then takes the results and recommendations to the faculty for further review and planning for school changes.

The *Instructional Walkthrough* model calls for a meeting of all teachers at the end of the school day. The team of observers, including building teachers, share observational notes to precipitate group discussion. The discussion promotes collegiality and the sharing of teaching ideas between those teachers who observed and those who were observed.

The walkthrough teams in the *Palisades School District Walkthrough* reconvene to share observations, strengths, and areas in need of attention regarding student learning. Their comments are summarized and shared with the faculty at an end-of-the-day meeting. All response sheets are left in the building for the principal/faculty teams to analyze and recommend changes in instructional materials and strategies by grade level and as a school.

Figure 9.1:
Variations on Classroom Walkthrough Feedback

Model	Feedback Process
Bristol Central High School Walk-Through	The walkthrough team discusses observations and decides on the form of follow-up, which can be either e-mail or face-to-face. A reflective question is often provided as part of feedback.
Data-in-a-Day (DIAD)	Research team members summarize findings and report back to all staff at the end of the school day.
Downey Three-Minute Classroom Walk-Through (CWT) with Reflective Practice	Reflective questions and conversations occur between observer and teacher. Conversation is aimed at moving teachers to self-reflection, self-analysis, and self-direction to change or improve the choice(s) they make as they teach.
Equity Learning Walk	Each member of the touring team discusses what s/he learned from the process and offers warm and cool follow-up to the host school team. The principal and school leadership team have options on how to share feedback with teachers.
Hall Walk-Through	At the end of the walkthrough, the administrator writes a brief, intentional, focused note on the *Hall Walk-Through Reflection Form* and leaves a copy on the teacher's desk. The follow-up is designed to guide the teacher into reflective practice.
High School Walkthrough	A written note or e-mail is provided to the teacher summarizing the evidence that supports the particular look-for. The visitor stops between classes to talk with the teacher about what was observed. Administrative team conducts debriefing to determine general patterns, which leads to the next level of staff development recommended for staff.
Instructional Practices Inventory (IPI) Process	Profiles of student engagement are provided for staff to collaboratively engage in the analysis and redesign of instruction using the IPI Process. Based on IPI profiles, next steps are recommended for structured study, analysis, reflection, and problem-solving.

Instructional Walkthrough	Notes are placed in teachers' mailboxes indicating key observations. The principal may make personal visits with teachers and/or hold a joint meeting of all teachers at the end of the school day to discuss what was observed.
Learning Keys' Data Walks	Data is shared as a composite picture of the building/ district only. Patterns of current instructional practice and student engagement are displayed. This data-driven composite is shared with the administration and school improvement team as a basis to identify needs, measure progress, and plan appropriate staff development.
The Learning Walk® Routine	The traditional methods for follow-up are The Learning Walk® follow-up letter sent by the principal to the entire school community or faculty or small group meeting. Teachers are presented with a summary of patterns and reflective questions, follow-up professional development topics, and information on the next learning walk.
Look 2 Learning (L2L) (formerly SMART Walks)	Cumulative, anonymous data is summarized and displayed graphically. Grade-level teams, departments, or professional learning communities can analyze and reflect on classroom trends and identify and monitor how to strengthen practices school-wide to improve student learning.
Mayerson Academy Classroom Walk-Through (CWT)	A follow-up sheet used by the observer provides descriptive notes about what was observed and raises questions to advance efforts to improve learning and instruction. If a group observed, they assemble to give an overview and specific evidence of what was seen, identify trends and areas of strength, and pose a reflective question.
(McREL) Power Walkthrough®	*(McREL) Power Walkthrough®* reports enable a school/ district to share the observations with teachers and coach them to higher levels of performance. A variety of reports help the administrator plan for coaching conversations and reflective questions for teachers and target staff development efforts.
Palisades School District Walk-through	The walkthrough team reconvenes about an hour before dismissal to share observations, strengths, and areas in need of attention. Comments are summarized and shared with the faculty at an end-of-the-day meeting.
School-Wide Walk-Through	Upon completing walks, visiting teams discuss their observations and findings. Capture sheets are used to

	share data at a voluntary debriefing held at the end of the day with all participants. Findings for areas of improvement are confidential and not discussed beyond the agreed-upon audience.
Teachscape Classroom Walkthrough (CWT)	Grade-level teachers and faculty committees examine the data to create a shared goal of improving instruction and boosting student achievement. Reflective discussions about the data lead to action planning that guides instruction and classroom practice.
UCLA SMP Classroom Walk-Through	Non-evaluative observation data is compiled and shared when the teams come together for a debriefing session. Reflective conversations follow to arrive at recommendations to further classroom practice that increases student understanding.
Walkthrough Observation Tool	A variety of strategies that meet the school's needs are recommended during debriefing with teachers and, in some instances, with students. Examples include oral and/or written follow-up, teacher reflection form, and meeting with faculty.

The *Instructional Practices Inventory (IPI) Process* provides the entire staff school-wide profiles of student-engaged learning. The IPI Process recommends a series of steps for purposeful, structured study, reflection, and problem-solving by all faculty based upon the IPI profiles. Teacher-leaders and the principal facilitate a whole-faculty collaborative study of the data. Working in small groups and then sharing out as a whole group, the faculty can move from developing a basic understanding of the categories of engagement to building images of more effective practices through the collaborative process. Rather than providing specific feedback to the staff, facilitators elicit faculty responses to the data. Faculty are asked to be reflective, inquiring learners and problem solvers and to integrate into their daily teaching experiences more meaningful, engaging learning experiences for their students. Organizational learning occurs as higher levels of collective faculty commitment and self-efficacy evolve from the collaborative study and support.

Several strategies are recommended for use in debriefing with teachers and, in some instances, with students when using the *Walkthrough Observation Tool*. This model begins by validating effective teaching and learning and encouraging its continued use. As the process develops, there are ample opportunities to engage teachers in discussion about areas for improvement. Sharing ideas and strategies encourages the initiation of learning communities among teachers.

> **Helpful Idea:** Avoid using the words "you" and "why" when framing the post-observation reflective questions. These words appear evaluative and are not conducive to reflective conversations.

A number of walkthrough models that enable observers to use walkthrough software for recording and storing observational data provide summarized follow-up data for school-wide review, reflection, and analysis. Those models include *Learning Keys' Data Walks, Look 2 Learning (L2L), (McREL) Power Walkthrough®* and *Teachscape Classroom Walkthrough (CWT).* Observation data can be uploaded to the Internet where observers can acquire charts, graphs, tables, and/or reports. This information can be specific to a building or can demonstrate trends throughout a district so that appropriate professional development can be planned. Refer back to Chapter Eight for details about software models.

In Summary

Follow-up from walkthroughs can be formal or informal, written or oral. Follow-up can be with an individual teacher, a grade-level or subject-level team, or the entire school faculty. To be most beneficial, follow-up will be a collegial discussion reflecting on teaching and learning observed and will be non-evaluative. As walkthroughs and the subsequent follow-up become part of a school culture, learning communities emerge and teachers take ownership for their professional growth.

As you reflect on your role as instructional leader in your school, consider the following:

- How will you provide follow-up to teachers?
- How can follow-up from classroom walkthroughs serve as an impetus for professional development and result in continuous improvement of teaching and learning?
- How can you use walkthrough follow-up to create a positive experience for all participants?

In Chapter Ten, we will address additional issues that you need to consider in preparing and introducing a new or revised walkthrough protocol in your school. We will provide recommended steps for implementing classroom walkthroughs.

10

Additional Factors to Consider about Classroom Walkthroughs

In this chapter, we will identify some of the additional factors that need to be considered if classroom walkthroughs are going to be viable in your school-improvement efforts. Careful planning is key and as with any new concept it is vital to consider what could hinder the success of the implementation of your walkthroughs. If you are in states with strong teacher unions, issues are almost certain to arise. Your planning process must include teacher participation and an evaluation of the protocol to develop the trust necessary for walkthroughs to succeed. As the school's instructional leader, you must manage your time well to remain consistent in conducting walkthroughs. We will address these issues and provide recommended steps and final thoughts on how best to implement classroom walkthroughs.

Naming the Process

We have encountered many names for what we have called "classroom walkthroughs" and numerous ways that they can be conducted. The name is less important than the fact that classroom walkthroughs, when carefully planned, implemented, and evaluated, will lead to instructional improvement and greater student achievement. However, some educators found that "classroom walkthroughs" conveyed a wrong image or intent that appeared as a top-down initiative. James Merrill, Superintendent of Virginia Beach City Public Schools, likes the descriptor "learning walks" to communicate to his teachers that he and his administrative cabinet enter classrooms to learn firsthand what is taking place, not to make judgments or evaluations about teachers.

Pam Robbins and Harvey Alvy name walkthroughs as *Leading and Learning by Wandering Around* (LLBWA). They portray one principal who hung a doorknob hanger on his office door that read, "Out Learning" while doing the walks. This sends a strong message that, for this principal, the walk was a high priority as well as a learning experience (Robbins & Alvy, 2004, p. 125). In some instances, schools call them "professional learning walks," again conveying the idea that professionals are in a school walking around learning from and sharing with one another.

Kim Marshall prefers to name short informal visits to the classrooms "mini-observations" rather than walkthroughs. To him, "classroom walkthroughs" leave the impression of walking through a classroom rather than pausing and observing thoughtfully (2009, p. 24).

As summarized by Ted Haynie, "Schools and districts can call it whatever they want but must adhere to the guiding principles that will ensure proper implementation" (T. Haynie, personal communication, June 24, 2009).

You must work with your faculty to decide what to call these walks. Like many of the other decisions about walkthroughs, the label you prefer will reflect the purpose of this effort and the outcomes expected.

> As a teacher, I knew that walkthroughs were not related to our formal evaluation process, which made the process very non-threatening. Knowing that our administrator had a vested interest in our school by wanting to know what was happening in our classrooms and by giving us informal praise for good teaching was invaluable. As teachers, we have our students' best interests in mind; with an administrator performing walkthroughs, being visible, and providing valuable input in regards to our teaching practices, we knew that she had the students' best interests in mind as well. We felt like a team and were able to meet the students' needs to our best ability.
>
> Sandy Linhart, Norwood Primary School,
> Norwood School District #63, Peoria, IL

Teacher Union Issues

The purpose of classroom walkthroughs must be transparent to all involved. Walkthroughs lend themselves to overall school efforts to improve student achievement; they are not designed for teacher evaluation. If, however, a district decides to use walkthroughs as part of the evaluation process, the school district/teacher union contracts will likely include language that spells out how and when information from any type of classroom walkthrough observations can be used in teacher evaluation. In any case, it is certainly desirable to involve your local teachers' union leadership in early discussions about walkthroughs. Teacher unions represent the rights of teachers, and they rightly wonder if walkthroughs are really evaluation in disguise, or as one educator shared with us, "stalk walks" rather than "learning walks."

Some elements of walkthroughs might become the subject of negotiated board/teacher union agreements:

- determination of the purpose of and look-fors in the walkthrough;
- teachers' involvement in walkthrough development;
- identification and training of participants in walkthroughs;
- indication or signal that the observer is conducting a walkthrough when entering classroom;
- timeframe for an abbreviated walkthrough;
- determination of when notations of observations can be recorded during the walkthrough;
- determination of the process for providing walkthrough feedback;
- assurance of confidentiality of walkthrough observation checklists/notations; and
- determination of what happens to any written or recorded documents from walkthroughs.

See Figure 10.1 for examples of provisions found in negotiated school/teacher contractual agreements.

Figure 10.1:
Negotiated Agreement Provisions on Classroom Walkthroughs

The Classroom Walk-Through shall not be used for performance or formal evaluation purposes. CWT will be conducted throughout the year by principals, assistant principals and district staff. Teachers will have CWT explained annually prior to the implementation of CWT. CWT data collection for individual teachers shall be confidential and shall not be placed in a teacher's personnel file.

TEACHER CONTRACT JULY 1, 2007 - JUNE 30, 2008 BETWEEN THE DISTRICT SCHOOL BOARD OF MONROE COUNTY, FLORIDA, AND THE UNITED TEACHERS OF MONROE

Walkthroughs provide administrators the opportunity to observe instructional patterns and encourage dialogue with teachers about teaching and learning. They raise the level of teacher awareness of exemplary teaching and learning practices. Walkthrough activity opens the door to coaching within the school. While administrators engage in walkthroughs, the message to staff should be clear regarding walkthrough purpose. Administrators must set the walkthrough purpose with the staff and view this activity as support and coaching and not evaluative. The walkthrough activity differs from classroom visitations that administrators engage in regularly.

WALKTHROUGHS (TEACHER PERFORMANCE APPRAISAL MANUAL, 2008) PINELLAS COUNTY SCHOOLS, FLORIDA

- *The purpose of classroom walkthroughs is to evaluate how the Illinois State Learning Standards are incorporated into daily lessons.*
- *Observers are encouraged to not only examine the walls and desks, but also a teacher's lesson plan book if one is readily available.*
- *Walkthroughs are 3 to 4 minutes; not any longer.*
- *Observers need to make it clear to the teacher that a classroom walkthrough is taking place.*
- *The observer is encouraged NOT to take notes during the walkthrough, but rather wait until after he/she has left the classroom to write his/her notes.*
- *Reflective questions should be delivered orally and in a neutral environment (NOT the principal's office) within 24 hours of the walkthrough.*

  AURORA WEST COMMUNITY UNIT SCHOOL DISTRICT #129, AURORA, ILLINOIS, AND AURORA EDUCATION ASSOCIATION-WEST

The ideal situation for walkthroughs is that they not become provisions within board-teacher negotiated agreements. Almost every one of the models cited in this book recommends that walkthroughs not be used for evaluative purposes because to do so will only reduce the flexibility and value of their use as a tool for improving teaching and learning. The real key is that school leadership creates a school culture whereby participants in walkthroughs are viewed as trusted, fair, and competent individuals who fulfill a supportive and guiding role. The context for walkthroughs should encourage and support teachers in risk-taking and support them with resources and feedback that result in new and effective teaching strategies.

Building Trust for Walkthroughs to Succeed

As emphasized in Chapter Four, building or enhancing trust in the relationship between teachers and between teachers and administrators represents a critical element in a collegial atmosphere where classroom walkthroughs are successful. Figure 10.2 lists five key components used to measure trustworthiness (Tschannen-Moran & Hoy, 1998, pp. 334–352) along with our recommendations on how to achieve trust in walkthrough situations.

David reiterates the importance of trust between the teacher and administrators. She says, "When the trust among teachers, principals, and central-office staff is low, walkthroughs are likely to be perceived as compliance checks" (2007–2008, p. 82). According to Deborah Tyler and her instructional walks, the most critical element of effective walks is trust. Classroom teachers should believe that walkthrough participants are a *support* to them, not a threat. Tyler is adamant that when teachers are part of creating the walkthrough protocol and deciding on the focus, trust is more likely to be present (ASCD, 2006).

A trusting relationship among all school community stakeholders creates a school culture that will promote academic success for all students. Classroom walkthroughs, when thoughtfully crafted and implemented, contribute to this culture.

The Reluctant Teacher and Walkthroughs

As indicated earlier in this book, a walkthrough protocol needs to become an essential part of the school culture where there is a continuous improvement effort in student learning. Yet, not all teachers are comfortable with visitors conducting walkthroughs in their classrooms. Until recently, teachers have

Figure 10.2:
Five Key Components of Trustworthiness and Walkthrough Recommendations

Components of Trustworthiness	Walkthrough Recommendations
Benevolence: A key ingredient to trust is that there is confidence that the other party has your best interests at heart and will protect your interests.	• Involve faculty in the design and implementation of walkthroughs. • Involve faculty in the evaluation of the walkthrough protocol.
Reliability: Reliability refers to the extent to which you can depend upon another party to come through for you, to act consistently, and to follow through.	• Be consistent in conducting walkthroughs. • Follow through by providing walkthrough feedback and commitments of support that arise from discussions with faculty.
Competence: Competence has to do with belief in another party's ability to perform the tasks required by his or her position. If a school leader means well but lacks necessary leadership skills, he or she is not likely to be trusted to do the job.	• Prepare for the walkthrough by working on skills of observation, active listening, leading reflective discussion, and awareness of best practices in teaching and learning. • Model what you expect of others.
Honesty: A person's integrity, character, and authenticity are all dimensions of trust. The degree to which a person can be counted on to represent situations fairly makes a huge difference in whether or not he or she is trusted by others.	• Be truthful in how all aspects of the walkthrough will be conducted and how data collected will be used. • Sincerely support teacher innovation and risk-taking as part of walkthroughs.
Openness: Judgments about openness have to do with how freely another party shares information with others. Guarded communication, for instance, provokes distrust because people wonder what is being withheld and why.	• Keep the entire walkthrough protocol transparent from beginning to end. • Keep information confidential when it needs to remain so. • Maintain visibility and accessibility through use of walkthroughs.

been relatively isolated in their work, and opening classrooms to observations and comments can increase feelings of anxiety and intimidation. This reluctance can work against the full-scale acceptance and implementation of walkthroughs.

Reluctance on the part of teachers can be caused by a lack of understanding about walkthroughs, lack of trust in those visiting the classrooms, or feelings of inadequacy or insecurity in their own teaching capabilities. Strategies that may help reduce anxiety follow:

- Involve teachers—including reluctant ones—in planning for walkthrough implementation.
- Be very sure that all teachers are clear as to the purpose and benefits of walkthroughs.
- Start classroom walkthroughs with teachers who are comfortable with the idea and have them share the benefits with those more reluctant.
- Invite teachers to accompany you as observers during walkthroughs.
- Assure that there is regular discussion about walkthroughs that includes an evaluation of the process and suggestions for improvement.
- Increase confidence by providing positive feedback on teachers' work and offering your support.

Managing Time to Conduct Walkthroughs

Chapter Six introduced the importance of creating time for walkthroughs. Some school leaders indicate that they would love to conduct walkthroughs, but they lack the time. That reasoning is synonymous with situations in which requests for items like professional development or school resources are turned down for lack of money. Lack of money and lack of time are not legitimate excuses. It really is the lack of priority. Like many of us who claim not to have time for physical exercise, walkthroughs will only occur when they are scheduled as part of the daily routine. Schedule walkthroughs as you would any other important entry into your calendar.

> **Helpful Idea:** Once teachers buy in to the value of walkthroughs, make sure the walks are continuously and consistently conducted.

Pete Hall acknowledges that as principal, one is naturally bombarded by demands from the central office, parent groups, faculty concerns, piles of e-mails, paper work, phone calls, and discipline issues. But he believes that if walkthroughs are a priority to your instructional leadership, many of the competing tasks can be completed after school (Hall, 2006). As Kim Marshall recalls,

> I found it most efficient to fit in my brief visits on the way to and from other errands and expeditions around the school. Sometimes I was successful in blocking out a whole period for classroom visits, but that amount of time rarely went by without my cell phone ringing or something else coming up. Still, with dogged persistence, it was usually possible to squeeze five visits into nooks and crannies of each day (Marshall, 2003, p. 704).

Some walkthrough models arrange for teachers to accompany the administrator in walkthroughs. In other models, teachers are the primary participants in the walks. While it may be difficult to arrange for teachers to be out of their classrooms to participate in walkthroughs, it depends on the purpose of the walkthroughs. If teachers can highly benefit professionally from participating, they should be included. The *UCLA SMP Classroom Walk-Through*, a teacher-led activity, recommends that a major role for the administrator is to champion the process and provide the needed support for it to occur. The administrators must have faith in the process and provide the teachers the time and freedom to work and learn together (Martinez-Miller & Cervone, 2008, p. 21).

Helpful Idea: Schedule informal walkthrough observations like you would any other important entry on your calendar.

Timothy Berkey recommends doing a "Leadership Audit" to capture snapshots of one's own daily leadership practices in order to study one's own habits. The audit (2009, p. 40) involves the collection of two types of data about oneself: (1) specific tasks performed throughout the workday (qualitative); and (2) time spent on each task (quantitative). He proposes that the audit can demonstrate where to change daily practices to invest more time in the improvement of teaching and learning. In other words, it redirects leadership to effective practices in instructional leadership—such as conducting walkthroughs.

Evaluating the Walkthrough Protocol

It is essential to step back throughout the walkthrough implementation process to determine if and how well the purposes are being met. Evaluation of the walkthrough should be formative in nature in order to affect improvement efforts for the school year. School leaders should take an active role in facilitating the evaluation. We suggest five areas of focus (see Figure 10.3) for evaluating the impact of walkthroughs on administrators, teachers, and students.

Those schools representing the grassroots models of classroom walkthroughs referenced in this book, Bristol Central High School, James Hubert Blake High School, and Palisades School District will attest that the walkthrough process in their respective sites is constantly evolving. Continuous evaluation of their effectiveness has resulted in modifications and enhancements that have made walkthroughs become an integral part of their school culture and school improvement efforts.

Figure 10.3:
Areas of Focus

Areas of Focus	Evaluation Questions
School culture and school climate	• Are trust, transparency, and truthfulness in conducting the walkthroughs evident in the school environment? • How do participants feel about the walkthrough?
Connections of walkthroughs with other school improvement initiatives	• How well is the classroom walkthrough working in concert with other school-improvement initiatives and strategies?
Components of the walkthrough protocol (e.g., frequency, timing, data collection, feedback)	• How are the various components of the walkthroughs working? • What are recommendations for improvement?
Support and resources for the success of the walkthroughs	• Are participants being provided time for conducting walkthroughs and giving feedback? • What professional development activities result from walkthrough feedback?
Value of walkthroughs to all participants	• Are all staff involved in and benefiting from the intended purpose and outcomes of the classroom walkthroughs? • How has participants' behavior changed as a result of walkthrough feedback? • How much progress has there been in student achievement that can be connected to the benefits of classroom walkthroughs?

Steps in Getting Started

Following are suggestions for planning and implementing classroom walkthroughs in your school building:

- Take time to thoroughly research the topic of walkthroughs to prepare for the many decisions to be made;
- Align classroom walkthroughs with other improvement and professional development efforts;
- Work with the faculty in deciding on the purpose of walkthroughs and the format of the walkthrough feedback;
- Research staff experiences with any previous walkthrough efforts;
- Send a team of teachers, teacher union representatives, and administrators to visit school districts that are successfully using classroom walkthroughs to improve teaching and learning;
- Provide for walkthrough training for all participants;
- Establish clear and consistent guidelines for those conducting walkthroughs and communicate those to the entire school community;
- Implement walkthroughs in the beginning on a voluntary basis allowing the early adopters of change to become advocates for the process and its value;
- Conduct formative evaluations of the walkthrough process regularly to determine what is working and what needs modification.

In Summary

Teacher participation in the design, implementation, and evaluation of the walkthrough process developed for your school is a must. Teacher involvement and careful planning are two important ingredients to assure that the walkthrough will be a successful tool in your efforts to improve teaching and learning. Other considerations include naming the walkthrough protocol you designed for your school, addressing teacher union contract issues, building a school culture of trust, working with reluctant teachers, managing time to schedule walkthroughs, organizing walkthrough protocols, and regularly evaluating the walkthrough process.

As you reflect on your role as instructional leader in your school, consider the following:

- What will you name your walkthrough process?
- Are there teacher-board contract issues you need to consider when planning to do walkthroughs?
- How are you building a culture of trust in your school to assure that walkthroughs will be successful?
- Which teachers might be reluctant to accept walkthroughs and how will you address them?
- How will you evaluate your walkthroughs?

Final Thoughts

It is apparent that there is no one right name for classroom walkthroughs or only one right way to conduct them. As Charlotte Danielson is quoted as saying, "There is no magic in the name of a model—only in the fidelity to the essentials of quality teaching" (Danielson, personal communication, July 3, 2009). Walkthroughs are valuable in helping instructional leaders acquire more accurate data regarding teaching, learning, and assessment in their classrooms.

It is important to study various walkthrough models and choose or create one that best fits your school's improvement efforts. Working together with teachers to define the purpose and develop that protocol for your school is critical as is the regular evaluation of your efforts.

Remember, the classroom walkthrough is a tool that can be used for different purposes, and its protocols can be adapted in various ways to meet these purposes. The ultimate goal is to open up the school—to increase sharing and to make teaching and learning a collaborative activity to increase student achievement.

Walk on to school improvement!

Appendix A: Classroom Walkthrough Model Executive Summaries/Contacts

Bristol Central High School Walk-Through

The purpose of the *Bristol Central High School Walk-Through* is to collect data on instructional effectiveness; provide relevant feedback to teachers, departments, and the school; create a school culture that encourages reflection and dialogue around effective instruction; and to identify professional development needs for each teacher, department, and/or school. Teachers are active participants in the walkthrough process. Department chairs (all teachers) participate as members of a walkthrough team with an administrator and curriculum specialist. The members of the walkthrough team witness instruction for five to ten minutes and then actively participate in a dialogue about what they observed with their team members. The feedback is meant to be non-evaluative encouragement for a teacher to reflect on a certain aspect of the learning process. For more information, contact Dr. Martin Semmel, Principal, Bristol Central High School, Bristol, Connecticut, at 860-584-7735, ext. 150 or at martinsemmel@ci.bristol.ct.us.

Data-in-a-Day (DIAD)

Data-in-a-Day (DIAD) is a tool that provides a short but intensive opportunity for a school to gather and report data about issues that both students and staff view as important. A facilitator usually works collaboratively with staff and students to select critical themes to observe at the school and then guides a group of staff, community members, and students to summarize data collected from the observation about those themes and present them back to the school. By including students and parents as active participants, the process enables a school to listen to students' voices about their own learning. For more information, contact Joan Shaughnessy now retired from the Northwest Regional Educational Laboratory (NWREL), Portland, Oregon, at 503-756-8738 or at joanshaughnessy@gmail.com.

Downey Three-Minute Classroom Walk-Through (CWT) with Reflection

The specific purpose of the informal *Downey Three-Minute Classroom Walk-Through (CWT) with Reflective Practice* is to help teachers learn to reflect proactively on teaching practices before implementing them in the classroom. More specifically, it is aimed at looking for curricular and instructional decisions teachers are making in the classroom. The approach is intended to enable each educator to become self-analytical and personally accountable for his or her work and to encourage educators to work collaboratively. The Downey CWT has two major parts: the observation and the reflective conversation. The observation is strictly observing, not judging or evaluating teachers. This model: (1) changes the professional relationships of the classroom supervisory practice; (2) changes the language of discourse itself by focusing on the relationships between teachers and principals; and (3) offers an approach to changing an entire school culture. For more information, contact Dr. Carolyn Downey at Palo Verde Associates, LaJolla, California, at 858-875-1333 or at cdowney@san.rr.com.

Equity Learning Walk (Kansas City, Kansas Public Schools)

The purpose of the *Equity Learning Walk* is to provide a school profile of equity in the school. Participants look for and note concrete examples that would reveal such equity. The protocol used for observations contains questions about the school and classroom environment, about teaching and learning, and about what to ask students during the visit. Areas of focus include racial, ethnic, and gender diversity; attention to different learning styles; relationships between students and learning styles; relationships between students and teachers; high expectations for all students; availability of resources to support different levels of language; and the use of differentiated instruction. Teachers and students are the focus of observations. Observers are asked to consider asking the teacher and students questions about content and understanding. For more information, contact Addie Hawkins, now retired from the Kansas City, Kansas Public Schools, at 913-334-6249 or at Addie.hwkns@yahoo.com.

Hall Walk-Through (Sheridan Elementary School, Spokane School District, Spokane, Washington)

The *Hall Walk-Through* is an observational tool designed to encourage self-reflection, build teacher capacity, and aid in the teacher evaluation process. An administrator needs to assure that everything within the school community is running smoothly. The model serves a dual utility for developmental and evaluative purposes. Useful "look-fors" in the walkthrough stem from intentionally focused discussions between the administrator and the teacher or teachers in question. Sometimes the entire school staff will agree on a certain "look-for" because it fits into the current focus of the school-wide improvement plan. At the end of the five-to-fifteen-minute classroom walkthrough, the administrator writes a brief, intentional, feedback-focused note on the Hall Walk-Through Reflection Form and leaves a copy on the teacher's desk on the way out. For more information, contact Pete Hall, Principal, Sheridan Elementary School, Spokane, Washington, at 208-755-3139 or at petehall@educationhall.com.

High School Walkthrough (Northern High School, Calvert County Public Schools, Prince Frederick, Maryland)

The *High School Walkthrough* is a two-to-five minute visit to classes throughout the school conducted on a frequent basis. Walkthroughs are informal and non-evaluative and are designed to find patterns in the data that can help members of the professional learning community to continually improve their teaching practices. Planning begins as look-fors are established by school leaders in concert with faculty and staff. The walkthroughs are conduced by the principal, other administrators, and/or teachers, depending on the school culture, and feedback to the teachers is informal. The final step is the debriefing with the planning team to discern the patterns from the observations and to determine the next steps. For more information about this particular walkthrough or others in use in Calvert County Public Schools, Prince Frederick, Maryland, contact Ted R. Haynie, retired Director of System Performance, Calvert County Public Schools, at 301-737-2500, ext. 311 or at tahaynie@towson.edu or reference *How to Conduct Effective High School Walkthroughs* DVD, Association for Supervision and Curriculum Development (ASCD).

Instructional Practices Inventory (IPI) Process

The *Instructional Practices Inventory (IPI) Process* provides the opportunity to systematically observe student engagement across the school setting and collaboratively study the engagement profiles as a faculty, both collectively and in small groups. From the reflective study (1) professional development can be identified, designed, and implemented; (2) engagement and instructional goals can be established; and (3) a common mission of improving student engagement, especially higher-order, deeper learning, can be embraced. The IPI allows principals and teachers to collaboratively and transparently monitor engagement and support school-wide instructional change. The collaborative study, reflection, and action were designed to foster a culture of professional community and organizational learning in support of continuous school improvement. For more information, contact Dr. Jerry Valentine, University of Missouri, Columbia, Missouri, at 573-882-0944 or at valentinej@missouri.edu.

Instructional Walkthrough

The *Instructional Walkthrough* is a brief non-evaluative visit to a classroom to take a structured look at the instructional practices, curriculum, assessment practices, and learning environment and how these impact student achievement. The faculty collaborates in identifying the "look-fors" that are part of the walkthrough. The observer is most often the school principal alone, but he/she may team up with a classroom teacher. For more information, contact Deborah Tyler, Director, Gatehouse Administration Center I, Fairfax County Public Schools, Fairfax, Virginia, at 571-423-1140 or at deborah.tyler@fcps.edu or reference *How to Conduct Effective Walk-Throughs* DVD, Association for Supervision and Curriculum Development (ASCD).

The Learning Keys' Data Walks

The Learning Keys' Data Walks provides data that can be recorded, stored, and shared in an electronic format to paint a picture of the current reality of instruction in a school. The protocol involves three-to-four minute visits during which the instructional process, student involvement and engagement, and classroom environment are measured based on a predetermined standard that has been shared with all staff members. For more information, contact Joe Crawford at jtcrawford@comcast.net or Learning Keys at 800-927-0478 or visit http://www.learningkeys.org.

The Learning Walk® Routine[1]

The Learning Walk® Routine: A Tool for Getting Smarter About Teaching and Learning is the Institute for Learning's signature tool. The routine consists of a set of professional activities organized around periodic walks through a school's halls and classrooms using the *Principles of Learning* to focus on the instructional core (how teachers teach, how students learn, and what gets taught to whom) and how the school or classroom is organized. On each walk a team of educators observes teacher and student talk and classroom artifacts to understand the extent to which professional development has influenced classroom practice and to consider next steps for professional development. The walks are a regular part of the work of the ongoing professional community. The Learning Walk® routine consists of embedded practices, norms, structures, and skills, all of which are taught to participants using The Learning Walk® Suite of Tools, an extensive collection of professional development resources. For more information, contact Nancy Israel, Institute for Learning, University of Pittsburgh, Pittsburgh, Pennsylvania, at 412-624-8319 or at nisrael@pitt.edu.

Look 2 Learning (L2L)

Look 2 Learning (L2L) is a research-based tool that allows schools to improve student achievement, generate data on learning, focus school improvement efforts, and begin discussions about improving classroom practices. The non-evaluative design of L2L makes it the ideal tool for peer coaches and team leaders, as well as school administrators. Training focuses

---

[1]The Learning Walk® © 2008 is the property of the Institute for Learning at the University of Pittsburgh and may not be used, reproduced, or distributed without the express written permission of the University of Pittsburgh. The Learning Walk® is a registered trademark of the University of Pittsburgh.

on reflective group analysis of curriculum alignment, levels of thinking, qualities of student work, learner engagement, and the instructional cycle. L2L can also be customized to monitor school and district initiatives. A Look 2 Learning software option provides an electronic way to collect information and send it to a web-based analysis program. The results are displayed graphically and comparatively to enable the school personnel to understand and target student learning issues for improvement. For more information, contact Lorie Garver, Colleagues on Call, at 877-411-6622 or lorie@411oncall.com or visit www.colleaguesoncall.com

Mayerson Academy Classroom Walk-Through (CWT)

The *Mayerson Academy Classroom Walk-Through (CWT)* is an organized visit through a school's learning area. Participants move in and out of classrooms looking at student work and artifacts and talking with students. The observers use an observation tool that focuses on students' learning. Between classroom visits, participants gather to discuss what they learned in the classroom by making objective statements and suggestions based on the evidence gathered. The purpose is threefold: (1) to develop a learning community focused on improving learning and instruction; (2) to involve teachers and the principal in a discussion about teaching and learning that meets the needs of all learners; and (3) to provide support of the vision that every child in every classroom can meet or exceed high standards. For more information, contact Kathleen T. Ware, President, Mayerson Academy, Cincinnati, Ohio, at 513-475-4100 or at ware.kathleen@mayersonacademy.org.

McREL Power Walkthrough®

The *McREL Power Walkthrough®* is a tool to help the administrator seek evidence that professional development and technology initiatives are actually taking place in the classroom and having impact on student performance. Participants in the McREL Power Walkthrough® need to have an understanding of the nine categories of instructional strategies from *Classroom Instruction That Works*. They also have to learn how to identify those strategies as practiced in the classroom. McREL Power Walkthrough® software helps school leaders turn their regular classroom observations into "power walkthroughs" by using a PDA, Tablet PC, Blackberry, or iPhone device loaded with McREL's web-based software. The software helps the observer focus on the observations of effective instructional strategies, student engagement, teachers' use of technology, and other factors that research shows to influence student learning. For more information, contact Howard Pitler, Senior Director of Curriculum and Instruction, Mid-continental Research for Education and Learning (McREL), Denver, Colorado, at 303-337-0990 or at hpitler@mcrel.org.

Palisades School District Walkthrough (Kintnersville, Pennsylvania)

The *Palisades School District Walkthrough* is designed to help learn more than standardized test scores tell about students and how successfully they are learning. Leadership teams at each school create their own questions to ask students in order to provide useful data. Their questions are connected to their instruction and content. Teams of visiting educators from outside of the school district (as well as some of the district's own educators, parents, and board members) engage students in the fall of the school year in one-on-one conversations about what they are learning. The walkthrough teams reconvene about an hour before dismissal to share observations, strengths, and areas in need of attention. These comments are summarized and shared with the faculty at an end-of-the-day meeting. The school then develops an improvement plan for implementation which will be reviewed by a second walkthrough in the spring. For more information, contact Dr. Francis V. Barnes, Superintendent of Schools, Palisades School District, Kintnersville, Pennsylvania, at 610-847-5131 or at fbarnes@palisadessd.org.

School-Wide Walk-Through (James Hubert Blake High School), Silver Spring, Maryland

The purpose of this collaborative *School-Wide Walk-Through* process is to create a system where all instructional staff work together to observe, discuss, and analyze teaching and learning to determine how student motivation is affected by the evidence of personal relationships, class climate, high expectations, and literacy support. A capture sheet is used by each visiting team member to write what he or she observed regarding teaching strategies or teachers' decisions in action in each of those categories. For more information, contact Moriah Martin, Staff Development Teacher, James Hubert Blake High School, Silver Spring, Maryland, at 301-879-1092 or at Moriah_A_Martin@mcpsmd.org.

Teachscape Classroom Walkthrough (CWT)

The *Teachscape Classroom Walkthrough (CWT)* is both a research-based process and a set of technology-enabled tools designed to help building administrators and others quickly collect data about classroom practice. Subsequently, they can use that information to work with teachers to plan and implement improvement and professional development activities. The CWT process engages instructional leaders and others in brief (four-to-seven minutes), frequent, structured classroom visits to gather and track instructional data as it relates to student performance. Data is collected on hand-held wireless devices and then uploaded to a web-based database where it is aggregated and displayed in a variety of customized graphic formats. These graphics are used as a guide for reflective discussions and action planning by the school community. The CWT process is, by design, transparent, inclusive, and focused on improving teaching practice to address the ultimate goal of the classroom walkthroughs—improving student achievement in every classroom. For more information, contact Maryann Marrapodi, Chief Learning Officer, at 212-336-0703 or at mmarrapodi@teachscape.com.

UCLA School Management Program (SMP) Classroom Walk-Through

The purpose of the *UCLA SMP Classroom Walk-Through* protocol is to help teachers gain a deeper understanding of their current practice and implement changes in practices that improve results. Classroom teachers are the primary participants of walkthroughs. The teachers decide on the results they want to influence; they communicate the instructional practices they want to change to improve student learning; they reflectively determine what areas of growth they need to undertake to improve their teaching effectiveness; and they determine the outcomes that measure their success. For more information, contact Laureen Cervone, Associate Director, Northeast Region, UCLA School Management Program at 203-365-8914 or at lcervone@smp.gseis.ucla.edu and Patricia Martinez-Miller, Director of Faculty, UCLA School Management Program at 310-420-9054 or at pmartine@smp.gseis.ucla.edu.

Walkthrough Observation Tool

The *Walkthrough Observation Tool* is a means for looking at the process of teaching and learning occurring in a school. It also provides a process for validating powerful teaching practices, effective use of guiding principles of learning, and the effective learning strategies demonstrated by students. Walkthrough participants observe student behaviors, their level of engagement, and the quality of their work. It is recommended that a variety of strategies be used for debriefing with teachers and in some instances with students. For more information, contact Dr. Otto Graf, Co-Director, Western Pennsylvania Principals Academy, School of Education, University of Pittsburgh, Pittsburgh, Pennsylvania, at 412-648-7119 or at <u>ograf@pitt.edu</u>.

Appendix B:
Classroom
Walkthrough
Models MATRIX

Model	Purpose	Observers
Bristol Central High School Walk-Through Bristol Central High School Bristol, CT	To collect data on instructional effectiveness; provide relevant feedback to school; create school culture that encourages reflection and dialogue on effective instruction; identify professional development needs.	Principal and assistant principals; department chairs and district curriculum coordinators; and/or teachers.
Data-in-a-Day (DIAD) Northwest Regional Educational Laboratory (NWREL) Portland, OR	To provide a short but intensive self-study opportunity for a school interested in gathering and reporting data about themes that both students and staff have determined as important for school improvement.	Students, parents, and teachers of the school serve as research teams for a one-time 24-hour day. In a school with 36 classrooms, 12 research teams visit three classrooms each.
Downey Three-Minute Classroom Walk-Through (CWT) with Reflective Practice Palo Verde Associates La Jolla, CA	To provide short, focused, informal observations that result in follow-up conversations for reflection, a focus on curriculum and instruction, and an informal and collaborative process.	Principal, coaches, mentors, and/or teachers.

Look-fors	Visit/ Frequency	Data Gathering	Feedback
Include objectives of lesson, learning environment, level of student engagement, choice of instructional activities, and student work.	Administrative teams conduct 10 classroom walks for about 5–10 minutes each. Department chair and district curriculum coordinator conduct walks twice a year.	The focus and related look-fors are dependent upon the group or individual conducting the walkthrough. Teams develop their own data gathering forms.	The walkthrough team discusses observations and decides on the form of follow-up, which can either be e-mail or face-to-face. A reflective question is often provided as part of feedback.
Based on the themes identified by the school that are often related to the school's improvement plan or professional development activities.	Research teams visit all of the classrooms in one day. Visits last a minimum of 20 minutes.	Research teams note specific examples of evidence that illustrate the key themes that are the focus of their walk. Observation instruments are developed specifically for each school using language students and parents can understand.	Research team members summarize findings and report back to all staff at the end of the school day.
Include five areas for observation: (1) student orientation to work; (2) curricular decisions; (3) instructional decisions; (4) walk the walls; and (5) health and safety conditions in the classroom.	Visits are from two to three minutes—as long as it takes to collect sufficient curriculum decisions. Frequency of visits is not interruptive to the classroom instructional period.	Observers may take notes for their own memory; however, no copy of notes is given to the teacher or placed in a file.	Feedback involves reflective questions and conversations between observer and teacher. Conversation is aimed at moving the teachers to self-reflection, self-analysis, and self-direction to change or improve the choices they make as they teach.

Model	Purpose	Observers
Equity Learning Walk Kansas City, Kansas Public Schools Kansas City, KS	To provide a school profile that would reveal equity in terms of instruction and opportunities for all students in the school.	Designed to be used by a team—principal, instructional coach, teachers, and others.
Hall Walk-Through Sheridan Elementary School Spokane, WA	To encourage self-reflection, build teacher capacity, and aid in the teacher evaluation process. The model serves a dual utility for developmental and evaluative purposes.	The school administrator or supervisors responsible for the development and evaluation of teachers.
High School Walkthrough Northern High School Prince Frederick, MD Featured in ASCD DVD titled "How to Conduct Effective High School Walk-throughs." Visit http://www.ascd.org/	To collect patterns of data on the application to classroom practices of knowledge and skills learned through professional development initiatives.	The high school's whole administrative team, principal and assistant principals.

Look-fors	Visit/ Frequency	Data Gathering	Feedback
Include attention to different learning styles, relationships between students and teachers, high expectations for all students, availability of resources to support different levels of language, and the use of differentiated instruction.	Visits are conducted once a semester or scheduled when changes have begun. Visits last 10 minutes at a maximum.	Observers record concrete examples of evidence revealing equity in the school.	Each member of the touring team discusses what s/he learned from the process and offers warm and cool feedback to the host school team. The principal and school leadership team have options on how to share feedback with teachers.
Stem from pre-observation conversations between the administrator and the teachers related to their own goals. They can also be from a grade-level team's goal or from the entire school staff.	Visits last from 5–15 minutes. The goal is to conduct intentional walkthrough visits of three to five different classrooms per day.	Observers use the *Hall Walk-Through Reflection Form* for narrative recordings.	At the end of the walkthrough, the administrator writes a brief, intentional, feedback-focused note on the Reflection Form and leaves a copy on the teacher's desk. The follow-up is designed to guide the teachers into reflective practice.
Based on the staff development teachers experienced. The administrative team identifies the specific look-fors.	5 x 5 Observation Method is used: Observers visit daily five classrooms for five minutes each and record five things observed.	Observers record five different pieces of information they have collected that show evidence of a new initiative within the school.	A written note or e-mail is provided to the teachers summarizing the evidence that supports particular look-fors. Administrative team conducts debriefing after at least 25 walks to determine general patterns of what was observed. This leads to the recommendation for the next level of staff development.

Model	Purpose	Observers
Instructional Practices Inventory (IPI) Process University of Missouri Columbia, MO	To increase engagement in meaningful learning by creating school-wide data profiles of student engagement for collaborative faculty study and problem-solving.	Best conducted by teacher-leaders in their respective schools. In some instances, principals, central office staff, and others may also serve as data collectors. IPI observers are required to be "certified" to collect data and facilitate faculty study of the data.
Instructional Walkthrough Eagle View Elementary School Fairfax, Virginia Featured in ASCD DVD titled "How to Conduct Effective Walkthroughs. " Visit http://www.ascd.org/	To maintain awareness of what is going on in classrooms throughout the school and to monitor the progress of specific school initiatives.	The school principal alone or teamed with classroom teachers.
Learning Keys' Data Walk Learning Keys Phoenix, AZ	To create a picture of the current reality of instruction in a building.	All administrative personnel within the district and building.

Look-fors	Visit/ Frequency	Data Gathering	Feedback
Focus on six coding categories on how students are engaged in learning activities. The observer is trained to understand the IPI coding process.	The observer moves from room to room throughout the school day and throughout the whole school collecting data, following the same systematic patterns so each classrom is observed multiple times. A typical obervation day can result in approximately 125–150 observations (1–3 minutes each), and with a minimum of 100 observations expected.	Data is gathered through the lens of the six IPI categories. For each category, there is a distinct way of codifying how the majority of the students in the learning setting are engaged.	Profiles of student engagement are provided for staff to collaboratively engage in the analysis and redesign of instruction using the IPI process. Based on IPI profiles, a series of steps is recommended for structured study, reflection, and problem-solving by all faculty.
Include instructional practices, curriculum, assessment practices, and learning environment and how these impact student achievement.	Visits usually last 5–10 minutes and are scheduled often enough that instruction continues and no one wonders why observers are there.	Observers make notes on a form that includes look-fors identifed by teachers.	Notes are placed in teachers' mailboxes indicating key observations. The principal may make visits with teachers and/or hold a joint meeting of all teachers at the end of the school day to discuss what was observed.
Focus on learner objectives; rate at which objectives are being addressed; assessment methods being used; research-based instructional strategies used; level of student engagement; and richness of learning enironment.	The protocol involves visits of 3–4 minutes during which the instructional process, student involvement and engagement, and classroom environment are measured based on a pre-determined standard which has been shared with all staff members.	Observations are recorded on a PDA or Blackberry so data can be uploaded to a desktop computer and then to the building/ district data system to electronically create reports sorted and separated by building, district, and date.	Data is shared as composite picture of the building/district only; never shared by classroom or teachers. The data is used to identify needs, measure progress, and plan staff development.

Model	Purpose	Observers
The Learning Walk® Routine Institute for Learning University of Pittsburgh Pittsburgh, PA	To inform decisions about professional development based on evidence of teaching and learning and to explore the extent to which new practices and content from professional development have found their way into classrooms.	Participants vary according to the learning needs of the participants and/or of the school staff. Learning walks may be led by administrators or teacher-leaders.
Look2Learning (L2L) (formerly SMART Walks) Colleagues on Call Phoenix, AZ	To improve student achievement by generating and analyzing data on rigor, relevance, and student engagement.	Principals, instructional coaches, and/or team leaders
Mayerson Academy Classroom Walkthrough (CWT) Mayerson Academy Cincinnati, OH	To: (1) develop a learning community focused on improving learning and instruction; (2) involve teachers and principals in a discussion about teaching and learning and meeting the needs of all learners; and (3) provide support for every child in every classroom to meet or exceed high standards.	Principals, teachers, counselors, central services, and board members.

Look-fors	Visit/ Frequency	Data Gathering	Feedback
Focus on one or more of the Institute's Nine Principles of Learning and is content-specific and generated from the professional development offered.	Participants spend 5–25 minutes in each of several classrooms looking at student work and classroom artifacts and talking with students and teachers.	Participants use an open-ended form that lends itself to notes about any type of evidence. The form identifies neither specific room numbers nor teachers and is for participants' use only.	The traditional method for feedback is The Learning Walk® letter sent by the principal to the entire school community. It includes a summary of patterns and reflective questions, follow-up professional development topics, and information on the next learning walk.
Focus on *student* learning, engagement, and work rather than *teaching*. Collected data includes high-impact, leading indicators of learning, analysis of curriculum alignment, levels of thinking, qualities of student work, learner engagement, and the instructional cycle.	Visits are 4 minutes and are frequent. Information about student learning, student engagement, and student work is collected.	Observers use a simple recording format, or they can collect the data electronically using L2L software on a PDA, smart phone, or desktop computer.	Cumulative, anonymous data is summarized and displayed graphically so grade-level teams, departments, and/ or professional learning communities can analyze and reflect on classroom trends and collaboratively identify and monitor how to strengthen practices school-wide to improve student learning.
Based on questions asked when interviewing students. These questions address rigorous content, higher-level thinking, student awareness of good work, and their ability to assess their own learning.	The length of the observation (usually about 5–10 minutes) is agreed upon in advance.	Observers use 3 forms: a CWT Building Summary form that has notes of what the observer saw/heard and recommendations for improvement; a form to determine use of Bloom's Taxonomy of thinking; and a student interview form for recording answers aimed at the students.	A follow-up sheet provides descriptive notes about what was observed and raises questions to advance efforts to improve learning and instruction. If a CWT group of observers are assembled, they give an overview and specific evidence of what was seen, identify trends, areas of strength, and pose a reflective question.

Model	Purpose	Observers
(McRel) Power Walkthrough® Mid-continent Research for Education and Learning (McRel) Denver, CO	To observe, evaluate, and record the extent to which teachers are using *Classroom Instruction That Works* strategies, the use of technology by teachers and students, levels of Bloom's Taxonomy, evidence of student learning, and other look-fors required by the district.	School and district administrators and curriculum directors and teachers.
Palisades School District Walkthrough Palisades School District Kintnersville, PA	To determine district-wide curricular changes and staff development needs by listening to students reveal how they learn, how teachers expect them to learn, and how they believe they could learn better.	Interview teams composed of the district's own educators, volunteers, parents, and school board members as well as educators from other schools and districts, and higher education.
School-Wide Walk-Through James Hubert Blake High School, Montgomery County Public Schools Rockville, MD	To unite all instructional staff to observe, discuss, and analyze teaching and learning to determine how educators' beliefs shape instructional decisions.	Every teacher in the high school. Teams are usually four people, each representing a different department, different levels, different experiences.

Look-fors	Visit/ Frequency	Data Gathering	Feedback
Relate to the nine strategies of *Classroom Instruction That Works* and teachers' and students' use of technology.	Visits are 3–5 minutes in duration in each classroom in the school.	Observations are recorded on a PDA, Tablet PC, IPhone, Blackberry, or device loaded with McREL's web-based software. Data is transmitted to the Internet to build reports/graphs of the school's instructional activity to determine the extent to which professional development is evident in classrooms.	*(McREL) Power Walk-through*™ reports enable a school/district to share the observations with groups or individual teachers and coach them to higher levels of performance. Several reports help the administrator plan for coaching conversations and post reflective questions for teachers and target staff development efforts.
Focus on interviewing students in one-on-one conversations about their learning, their awareness of the standards used to create it, how their work is evaluated, and how to improve it.	Interviews typically take about 15 minutes and are guided by a consistent set of questions that have been compiled jointly by teachers and administrators.	Observers record student responses to specific questions. Student responses are documented and summarized for both quantitative and qualitative analysis.	The walkthrough team reconvenes about an hour before dismissal to share observations, strengths, and areas in need of attention. Comments are summarized and shared with faculty at an end-of-the-day meeting.
Focus on student motivation by observing teaching strategies or decisions in action in each of the categories of classroom climate, relationships, literacy, and expectations.	Each group visits 3 or 4 assigned classrooms for 7–10 minutes each.	A capture sheet is used for visiting team members to write what they observed regarding teaching strategies or teachers' decisions in each of the categories of classroom climate, relationships, literacy, and expectations.	Upon completing walks, visiting teams discuss their observations and findings. Capture sheets are used for sharing data at a voluntary debriefing held at the end of the day with all participants invited. Areas of improvement are confidential.

Model	Purpose	Observers
Teachscape Classroom Walkthrough (CWT)	To improve student achievement by improving the instructional practices that shape student learning.	Instructional leaders—principals, assistant principals, department heads, coaches, and lead teachers. At the discretion of the school or district, other professionals may conduct the walks.
UCLA SMP Classroom Walk-Through	To help teachers gain a deeper understanding of the results of their current practice and implement the kind of changes to improve practice that improves results.	Teams of classroom teachers are the primary participants of the walkthroughs.
Walkthrough Observation Tool Principals Academy of Western Pennsylvania University of Pittsburgh Pittsburgh, PA	To see the school in operation and to begin collecting base-line data around a spectrum of effective instructional practices.	Principal, teachers, and others.

Look-fors	Visit/ Frequency	Data Gathering	Feedback
Include elements of research-based practices in use of questioning, student engagement, categories of effective instructional strategies, and degree of differentiation.	School determines frequency and length of time for walkthroughs. Visits range from 4–7 minutes.	Using the Teachscape software, walkers record data on a handheld device. Data is then transmitted to the Internet to build a picture of the school's instructional activity. The data may be shaped into reports and graphs.	Grade-level teachers and faculty committees examine the data to create a shared goal of improving instruction and boosting student achievement. Reflective discussions about the data lead to action planning that guides instruction and classroom practice.
Focus on evidence of student learning impacted by instructional or curricular initiatives, assessment efforts, or professional development.	Visits are 5–7 minutes in each classroom. The frequency is determined by the purpose. It is recommended that they occur no less than once a month.	Observers record their observations without interpretation and connect those observations with any notes, thoughts, and questions. There are no checklists.	Non-evaluative observation data is compiled and shared in a debriefing session with teachers by the next day. Patterns seen within and across classrooms are noted. Reflective conversations among school staff follow to arrive at recommendations to further classroom practice that increases student understanding.
Include students' learning behaviors and products, level of engagement, and quality of work.	Number of visitations may vary, but usually 8–12 classroom visits of approximately 5 minutes each.	Specific examples of effective practice and exact details about the implementation/use of effective instruction are recorded.	A variety of strategies is used for debriefing with teachers and in some instances with students. Examples include oral and/or written follow-up, teacher reflection form, and meeting with faculty.

Appendix C:
Planning Template: Classroom Walkthroughs in Your School/District

Informal Classroom Observations

How will teachers be involved in the design and implementation?

What will be the purpose of the walkthough?

Who will participate as observers in this process?

What will be the focus of observations in the walkthrough?

How much time will be spent with a visit? How often will visits be conducted?

Data Collection Techniques and Approaches

What will be recorded from the walkthrough?

How will data from the walkthrough be recorded (e.g., checklist, narrative form, handheld device?)

Follow-up Observations

What will be shared with others from the walkthrough?

How will data be shared with others from the walkthrough?

Appendix D:
Learning Walk Newsletter

Midwood High School at Brooklyn College
LEARNING WALK NEWSLETTER

Why do we Walk? ~ The Mission of the Learning Walk Teams

The learning walk teams expect to foster the development of a professional learning community at Midwood High School. Through **non-evaluative** walkthroughs, the teams plan to gather and share teaching strategies as well as advance on-going dialogue pertaining to instructional methodologies.

What have we done?

After 3 sessions of conversations and considering the suggestions made on election day, the learning walk teams have created the following assumptions for our visits:

- Monthly, each group will focus on a specific instructional technique determined by a convener.
- Each group will split into sub-groups of 2-4 members when visiting classes.
- Each member will note objective evidence of the highlighted instructional technique.
- The team will meet to share the data collected. While sharing this data, each group member is expected to avoid judgment and/or evaluation. Our focus is to observe teaching methodologies and not teachers themselves.
- Team members will provide non-evaluative feedback/recognition to the teachers whose classes we visit.
- The Learning Walk Newsletter will be created and distributed to the faculty periodically. Each newsletter will contain samples of the data collected (void of names).

December's walks:

With a focus on active participation, the following examples were noted during our December walks:

- Student told a team member "every student is involved in a different group"
- While entire class was engaged in an activity, students were able to talk quietly with their neighbor for assistance.
- Classes seated in U-shape promoted conversation and accountable talk.
- Teacher quoted as saying "**Everybody** take out your books."
- Teacher quoted as saying "...think about it. (pause) Do it on your paper"
- Each student in a group was assigned a unique task.
- Teacher prompted class to write a paragraph "about the importance of religion in ritual and in life. Then we will talk about it."
- Class seated in groups of 4 and each group was asked to explore a unique aspect of a broader topic.
- Class responds in unison to teacher prompts.

Learning Walk Team Members:
Period 6 ~
Period 7 ~

If you have questions or concerns, please discuss with any of the Learning Walk Team Members.

Appendix E:
Walkthrough Feedback Letter

Martin Luther King, Jr. Middle School
4545 Ammendale Road
Beltsville, Maryland 20705
www.pgcps.pg.k12.md.us/~mlkms

301.572.0650 (Main Office)
301.572.0660 (Guidance Office)
301.572.0668 (Fax)

Robin J. Wiltison
Principal

November 3, 2008

Dear MLK Staff,

At this extremely busy time of year, I greatly appreciate your willingness to allow your colleagues and the Hyattsville Middle School team to visit your classrooms. The teachers whose classes were visited are to be commended for their commitment to the instructional best practices associated with the Institute for Learning (IFL). Criteria which supported the focus of the Learning Walk, Clear Expectations, were evident throughout the building. Specific "look fors" included: Students can show you examples of their work and describe the criteria they are trying to meet. Teacher feedback is given to students in terms of the standards and rubrics.

The comments shared by the five teams, during the debriefing session, supported your professional growth in Clear Expectations. Specific observations regarding our math program were teased out for further reflection. It was said by many, "I have learned from visiting my colleagues' classrooms and I will be 'borrowing' strategies that I observed." There is no higher validation of your work than a colleague's praise. The following are key observations and wonderings associated with our staff's growth in the area of Clear Expectations.

Standards that include models of student work are available to and discussed with students:

- Posted student work had specific comments for improvement on post-it notes.
- Hallways had samples of work using the criteria of good, better, best.

Students judge their work with respect to the standards:

- There was evidence of rubrics in most classrooms, teacher and student created.
- Student - teacher conferences were observed.

Intermediate expectations leading to the formally measured standards are specified:

- Students were familiar with rituals and routines and understood the expected lesson outcomes.
- Math notebooks were organized and the students articulated in such a way that demonstrated higher order thinking.

Families and community are informed about the accomplishment standards that all children are expected to achieve:

- Agenda books with homework and parent communication pages were visible.
- Grade factor sheets were posted; science fair packets and safety contracts were signed by parents.
- Gallery walks and project presentations allowed for opportunities for students to explain their work.

Wonderings included:

- I wonder if students self select items for their portfolios.
- I wonder if students understand the learning purpose of posted graded work.
- I wonder how instruction is differentiated for students.
- I wonder if explicit comments on posted work would assist students in the learning process.
- I wonder if increasing wait time would allow for students to provide quality feedback on what was learned.
- I wonder how and when rubrics are created in the classrooms.
- I wonder if rubrics are incorporated in every class, especially creative arts.
- I wonder if the posted work is current since it was not dated

Math specific wonderings:

- I wonder how often gallery walks are held and how successful they are in improving student work.
- I wonder if the skills needed to complete the math project are from the first quarter curriculum.
- I wonder why students are not showing the steps/process when completing math work.
- I wonder if students have any input in the grading of projects.

The Learning Walk process provided a glimpse into the instructional practices of the school. The walkers' feedback not only revealed areas of growth, since the previous walks, but also patterns where professional development will be helpful. It is apparent from this Learning Walk that the staff would benefit from professional development in the following areas:

- The effective development and use of rubrics
- How to provide explicit feedback on student work
- Posting student work as a learning tool for others
- Writing differentiated objectives, followed by differentiated instruction

Again, thank you for allowing us to visit your classrooms. In spite of the fact that learning walks may feel like an evaluative process, they are designed to help us discover what students are hearing, learning and producing as we focus on important core content. As a staff we are making excellent progress in our IFL work.

Sincerely,

Robin J. Wiltison

References

Abrutyn, L. S. (2006). The most important data. *Educational Leadership.* 63 (6), 54–57.

Alberta Teachers' Association. (2006). A guide to the classroom walk-through. *Issues for Administrators Series.* Monograph #13.

Archer, J. (2005). Educators see classroom visits as powerful learning tools. *Education Week.* 24 (43), 22–24.

ASCD. (2006). *How to conduct effective classroom walk-throughs.* Alexandria, VA: Association for Supervision and Curriculum Development.

ASCD. (2007). *How to conduct effective high school classroom walk-throughs.* Alexandria, VA: Association for Supervision and Curriculum Development.

Aurora Education Association-West. (2009). *Information about classroom walkthroughs.* Illinois Education Association, v3.1.0. Retrieved July 10, 2009, from http://www.ieanea.org/local/aeaw/content.asp?active_page_id=153.

Barnes, F., & Miller, M. (2001a). Data analysis by walking around. *The School Administrator.* 58 (4), 20–22, 24–25.

Barnes, F., Miller, M., & Dennis, R. (2001b). Face to face. *Journal of Staff Development,* 22 (4), 42–43, 47.

Berkey, T. B. (2009). *Improving your daily practice: A guide for effective school leadership.* Larchmont, NY: Eye on Education.

Black, S. (2007). Making the rounds. *American School Board Journal,* 194 (12), 40–41, 45.

Blatt, B., Linsley, B., & Smith, L. (2005). Classroom walk-throughs their way. *UCLA SMP EdNews* Retrieved (July 7, 2009), from http://www.smp.gseis.ucla.edu/Resourcesforyou/ednews/ednews_2005_01.html

Bloom, G. (2007). Classroom visitations done well. *Leadership,* 36 (4), 40–42, 44–45.

Brinkman, A., Forlini, G., & Williams, E. (2009). *Help teachers engage students: Action tools for administrators.* Larchmont, NY: Eye On Education.

Brockton Public Schools. (2008). *District plan for school intervention.* Retrieved March 18, 2009, from http://www.doe.mass.edu/boe/docs/0508/0044dplan.pdf.

Center for Comprehensive School Reform and improvement/Learning Point Associates Newsletter. *Using the classroom walk-through as an instructional leadership strategy*. (2007). Retrieved March 19, 2009, from http://www.centerforcsri.org/fles/TheCenter_NL_Feb07.pdf.

Cervone, L., & Martinez-Miller, P. (2007). Classroom walkthroughs as a catalyst for school improvement. *Leadership Compass*. 4 (4). Retrieved May 27, 2009, from http://www.naesp.org/resources/2/Leadership_Compass/2007/LC2007v4n4a2.pdf.

Collins, J. (2001). *Good to great: Why some companies make the leap...and others don't.* New York: HarperCollins Publishers, Inc.

Collins, J.A. (2009). *Higher-order thinking in the high-stakes accountability era: Linking student engagement and test performance.* Unpublished doctoral dissertation. University of Missouri, Columbia, MO.

Connecticut walkthrough protocol guide (2008). Connecticut Department of Education. Retrieved May 22, 2009, from http://www.sde.ct.gov/sde/lib/sde/pdf/Curriculum/Walkthrough_Protocol_Guide_2008.pdf

Cotton, K. (2003). *Principals and student achievement: What the research says.* Alexandria, VA: Association for Supervision and Curriculum Development.

Craig, B. (2006). My recipe for school improvement: Walk-through observations on a handheld computer. *The Administrative Observer*. Retrieved June 11, 2009, from http://www.pes-sports.com/pe06000.htm.

Cronk, D., Inglis, L., Michailides, D., Michailides, M., Morris, D, & Petersen, N. (2009). Walking the talk: Instructional talk throughs. *The ATA News* 43 (3), 1–3.

Danielson, C. (2009). *Talk about teaching! Leading professional conversations.* Thousand Oaks, CA: Corwin Press.

David, J. L. (2007–2008). What research says about...classroom walk-throughs. *Educational Leadership*. 65 (4), 81–82.

Dexter, R. (Spring 2005). Classroom walk-through with reflective feedback: Principals' perceptions of the learning 24/7 classroom walk-through model. *National Forum of Educational Administration and Supervision Journal*, 22 (3), 24–39.

Downey, C. J., Steffy, B. E., English, F. W., Frase, L. E., & Poston, Jr., W. K. (2004). *The three-minute classroom walk-through: Changing school supervisory practice one teacher at a time.* Thousand Oaks, CA: Corwin Press.

Downey, C. J. (2008). *Classroom walk-throughs*, Chapter Eight in *Powerful Designs for Professional Learning*, Second Edition, (L. B. Easton, Ed.). Oxford, OH: National Staff Development Council. 95–106.

Downey, C. J., Steffy, B. E., Poston, W. K. Jr., & English, F. W. (2009). A*dvancing the three-minute walk-through: Mastering reflective practice.* Thousand Oaks, CA: Corwin Press.

DuFour, R., DuFour, R., Eaker, R., & Many, T. (2006). *Learning by doing: A handbook for professional learning communities that work.* Bloomington, IN: Solution Tree.

DuFour, R., & Marzano, R. J. (2009). High leverage strategies for principal leadership. *Educational Leadership*. 66 (5). 62–68.

Easton, L. B. (2008). *Powerful designs for professional learning* (2nd ed.). Oxford, OH: National Staff Development Council.

Elmore, R. F. & Burney, D. (1997). *Investing in teacher learning: Staff development and* instructional improvement in community school district #2, New York City. CPRE Research contract #R11G10007 with the Office of Educational Research and Improvement of the U.S. Department of Education. Retrieved June 24, 2009, from http://www.nctaf.org/documents/archive_investing-in-teacher-learning.pdf.

Fink, E., & Resnick, L. B. (2001). Developing principals as instructional leaders. *Phi Delta Kappan.* 82 (8), 598–606.

Fleck, F. (2005). *What successful principals do! 169 tips for principals.* Larchmont, NY: Eye On Education.

Frase, L. E. (2001). *A confirming study of the predictive power of principal classroom visits on efficacy and teacher flow experiences.* Presentation at the Annual meeting of the American Educational Research Association, Seattle, WA.

Frase, L. E., & Hetzel, R. (2002). *School management by wandering around.* Lancaster, PA: Technomic Publishing, Inc. (1990, reprinted 2002).

Fullan, M. (1999). *Change forces: The sequel.* London: Falmer Press.

Ginsberg, M. B., & Murphy, D. (2002). How walkthroughs open doors. *Educational Leadership.* 59 (8), 34–36.

Goldman, P., et.al. (2008). *The learning walk*[TM] *sourcebook.* Institute for Learning, Learning Research & Development Center, University of Pittsburgh.

Graf, O., & Werlinich, J. (2002). *Observation frustrations...Is there another way? The walkthrough observation tool.* Unpublished paper. University of Pittsburgh: Principals Academy of Western Pennsylvania.

Gray, S. P., & Streshly, W. A., (2008). *From good schools to great schools: What their principals do well.* A Joint Publication by the National Association of Elementary School Principals and Corwin Press. 109–110.

A guide to the classroom walk-through. (2006). Issues for Administrators Series. Monograph #13.

Hall, G. E., & Hord. S. M. (2000). *Implementing change: patterns, principles, and potholes.* Boston: Allyn & Bacon.

Hall, Pete (2006). Get Out of That Chair! *Education World.* Retrieved June 20, 2009 from http://www.education-world.com/a_admin/columnists/hall/hall006.shtml.

Hall, P., & Simeral, A. (2008). *Building teachers' capacity for success: A collaborative approach for coaches and school leaders.* Alexandria, VA: Association for Supervision and Curriculum Development.

Hallinger, P. (2007). *Leadership for learning. Reflections on the practice of instructional and transformational leadership.* Presentation at the Australian Council for Educational Research, Melbourne, Australia. Retrieved July 12, 2009, from http://www.acer.edu.au/documents/RC2007_Hallinger-Presentation.pdf.

Harris, S. (2006). *Best practices of award-winning secondary school principals.* A Joint Publication by the National Association of Secondary School Principals and Corwin Press.

Hord, S. M. (2004). *Learning together, leading together: Changing schools through professional learning communities.* A Joint Publication by Teachers College Press and National Staff Development Council.

Hord, S. (2009). Professional learning communities: Educators work together toward shared purpose—Improved student learning. *Journal of Staff Development.* 30 (1), 40–43.

Hord, S. M., & Sommers, W. A. (2008) *Leading professional learning communities: Voices from research and practice.* A Joint Publication by the National Association of Secondary School Principals and Corwin Press.

Interstate school leadership licensure consortium standards for school leaders. (2008). Washington, D.C.: Council of Chief State School Officers.

Johnson, J. (2001). Leadership by walking around: Walkthroughs and instructional improvement. *The Principals; Partnership.* Retrieved July 28, 2009, from http://www.principalspartnership.com/feature203.html.

Kerr, K. A., Marsh, J. A., Ikemoto, G. S., Darilek, H., & Barney, H. (2006). Strategies to promote data use from instructional improvement: Actions, outcomes, and lessons from three urban districts. *American Journal of Education.* 112 (4), 496–520.

Keruskin, T. (2005). *The perceptions of high school principals on student achievement by conducting walkthroughs.* Unpublished doctoral dissertation, University of Pittsburgh, Pittsburgh, PA.

Killion, J. P. & Todnem, G. R. (1991). A process for personal theory building. *Educational Leadership.* 48 (6), 14–16.

Knowles, M. S., Holton, E.F., & Swanson, R.A. (1998). *The adult learner: The definitive classic in adult education and human resource development.* Houston, TX: Gulf Publishing.

Lambert, L. (2002). A framework for shared leadership. *Educational Leadership.* 59 (8), 37–40.

Langer, J. A. (2000). Excellence in English in middle and high school: How teachers' professional lives support student achievement. *American Educational Research Journal.* 37(2), 397–439.

Larson, K. (2007). Developing reflective practice through snapshots of teaching and learning. *Leadership Compass.* 4 (4). Retrieved April 21, 2009, from http://www.naesp.org/resources/2/Leadership_Compass/2007/LC2007v4n4a3.pdf

Lawler, P. A. (1991). *The keys to adult learning: Theory and practical strategies.* Philadelphia, PA: Research for Better Schools.

Lemons, R. W., & Helsing, D. (2009). Learning to walk, walking to learn: Reconsidering the walkthrough as an improvement strategy. *Phi Delta Kappan.* 90 (7). 479–484.

Maloy, K. (1998). *Building a learning community: The story of New York City community school district #2.* Learning and Research Development Center, University of Pittsburgh. Research contract #RC–96–137002 with the Office of Educational Research and Improvement at the U.S. Department of Education. Retrieved May 22, 2009, from http://www.lrdc.pitt.edu/hplc/publications/building%20portrait.pdf.

Mandell, E. (2006). *Supervisory practices and their effect on teacher's professional growth.* Unpublished doctoral dissertation, University of Pittsburgh, Pittsburgh, PA.

Marshall, K. (2003). Recovering from HSPS (Hyperactive superficial principal syndrome): A progress report. *Phi Delta Kappan.* 84 (9), 701–709.

Marshall, K. (2009). Mini-observations—Seven decision points for the principal. *Education Week.* 28 (20), 24–25.

Martinez-Miller, P., & Cervone, L. (2008). *Breaking through to effective teaching: A walk-through protocol linking student learning and professional practice.* Lanham, MD: Rowman & Littlefield Education.

Marzano, R. J., Pickering, D. J., & Pollock, J. E. (2001). *Classroom instruction that works: Research-based strategies for increasing student achievement.* Alexandria, VA: Association for Supervision and Curriculum Development.

Marzano, R. J., Waters, T., & McNulty, B. (2005). *School leadership that works: From research to results.* Alexandria, VA: Association for Supervision and Curriculum Development.

Merrill, R. A. (2008). *Attitudes toward and use of classroom walkthroughs in Illinois schools.* Carbondale, IL: Southern Illinois University.

O'Rourke, A. O., Provenzano, J., Bellamy, T., & Ballek, K. (2007). *Countdown to the principalship: A resource guide for beginning principals.* Larchmont, NY: Eye On Education.

Penuel, W. R., Chung, M. & Gorges, T. (2007) A PD3 tool for observing mathematics and science instruction. *Leadership Compass.* 4 (4). Retrieved June 18, 2009, from http://www.naesp.org/resources/2/Leadership_Compass/2007/LC2007v4n4a1.pdf.

Peters, T. J., & Austin, N. (1985). *A passion for excellence: The leadership difference.* New York: Random House.

Peters, T. J., & Waterman, Jr., R. H. (1982). *In search of excellence: Lessons from America's best-run companies.* New York: Harper & Row.

Pinellas County Schools. (2008). *Teacher performance appraisal manual.* Retrieved (April 18, 2009), from http://www.nctq.org/evaluation_handbook/18-07.pdf.

Pink, D. H. (2006). *A whole new mind: Why right-brainers will rule the future.* New York: Riverhead Trade.

Pitler, H., & Goodwin, B. (2009). Classroom walk-throughs: Learning to see the trees and the forest. *The Learning Principal.* National Staff Development Council. 4 (4), 1, 6–7.

Pitler, H., Hubbell, E. R., Kuhn, M., & Malenoski, K. (2007). *Using technology with classroom instruction that works.* Alexandria, VA: Association for Supervision and Curriculum Development.

Principles of Learning. (2007). Institute of Learning, University of Pittsburgh. Retrieved May 22, 2009 from http://ifl.lrdc.pitt.edu/ifl/index.php?section=pol.

Protheroe, N. (2009). Using classroom walkthroughs to improve instruction. *Principal.* 88 (4) 30–34.

Richardson. J. (2001). Seeing through new eyes: Walk throughs offer new way to view schools. *Tools for Schools.* Oxford, OH: National Staff Development Council.

Rissman, L. M., Miller, D. H., & Torgesen, J. K. (2009). *Adolescent literacy walk-through for principals: A guide for instructional leaders.* Portsmouth, NH: RMC Research Corporation, Center on Instruction.

Robbins, P., & Alvy, H. (2004). *The new principal's fieldbook: Strategies for success.* Alexandria, VA: Association for Supervision and Curriculum Development.

Rossi, Guy. (2007). *The classroom walkthrough: The perceptions of elementary school principals on its impact on student achievement.* Unpublished doctoral dissertation. University of Pittsburgh, Pittsburgh, PA.

Salter, S., & Walker, M. (2008). Leading staff renewal through instructional leadership strategies of looking at student work protocols and principal led walkthroughs. Retrieved July 28, 2009, from http://www.acel.org/au/fileadmin/user_upload/documents/conference_2008/papers/Salter-Walker.doc

Sather, S. E. (2004). *The Spokane School District: Intentionally building capacity that leads to increased student achievement.* Portland, OR: Northwest Regional Educational Laboratory.

Schlechty, P. C. (2001). *Shaking up the school house: How to support and sustain educational innovation.* San Francisco, CA: Jossey-Bass.

Schmoker, M. (2006). *Results now: How we can achieve unprecedented improvements in teaching and learning.* Alexandria, VA: Association for Supervision and Curriculum Development.

School Change Collaborative (2000). *Listening to student voices: Data in a day Guidebook.* Laboratory Network Program. Portland, OR: Northwest Regional Educational Laboratory.

Skretta, J., & Fisher, V. (2002). The walk-through crew. *Principal Leadership.* 3 (3), 39–41.

Smith, J. B., Lee, V. E., and Newmann, F. M. (2001). *Improving Chicago's schools: Instruction and achievement in Chicago elementary schools.* University of Chicago, Consortium on Chicago School Research.

Steiny, Julia. (2009). Learning walks: Build hearty appetites for professional development. *Journal of Staff Development.* 30 (2), 31–32, 34, 36.

Stronge, J. H., Richard, H. B., & Catano, N. (2008). *Qualities of effective principals.* Alexandria, VA: Association for Supervision and Curriculum Development.

Supovitz, J. A., & Poglinco, S. M. (2001). *Instructional leadership in a standards-based reform.* Philadelphia, PA: Consortium for Policy Research in Education.

Tanner-Smith, T., Jordan, G., Kosanovich, M., & Weinstein, C. (2009). *Principal's reading walk-through: Kindergarten–grade 3 participant's guide.* Portsmouth, NH: RMC Research Corporation, Center on Instruction.

Teacher contract between the district school board of Monroe County, Florida and the United Teachers of Monroe. (July 1, 2007 – June 30, 2008). Retrieved July 14, 2009, from http://www.utmonline.org/Final%20Teacher%20Contract%202007-2008.pdf.

Tomlinson, C. A. (1999). *The differentiated classroom: Responding to the needs of all learners.* Alexandria, VA: Association for Supervision and Curriculum Development.

Tschannen-Moran, M., & Hoy, W.K. (1998). Trust in schools: A conceptual and empirical analysis. *Journal of Educational Administration, 36*(4), 334–352.

Valentine, J. W. (2007). *The instructional practices inventory: Using a student learning assessment to foster organizational learning.* Retrieved April 27, 2009, from http://education.missouri.edu/orgs/mllc/Upload%20Area-Docs/IPI%20Manuscript%2012-07.pdf

Valentine, J. W., & Collins, J. A. (2009). *Analyzing the relationships among the instructional practices inventory, school culture and climate, and organizational leadership.* Presentation at the American Educational Research Association, San Diego, California April 14, 2009.

Valli, L., & Buese, D. (2007). The changing roles of teachers in an era of high-stakes accountability. *American Educational Research Journal.* 44 (3), 519–558.

Walk-throughs are on the move. (2008). Education World®. Retrieved July 24, 2009, from http://www.educationworld.com/a_admin/admin/admin405.shtml.

Walker, K. (2005). Walkthroughs. Research brief. *The Principals' Partnership.* Retrieved June 19, 2009, from http://www.principalspartnership.com/walkthroughs.pdf.

Weber, S. (2007). In the real world: The many benefits of classroom walkthroughs. *Leadership Compass.* 4 (4). Retrieved June 25, 2009, from http://www.naesp.org/resources/2/Leadership_Compass/2007/LC2007v4n4a4.pdf.

What school leaders need to know about walk-throughs (2006). *The Learning Principal.* 1 (5), 4–5. National Staff Development Council.

Whitaker, T., & Zoul, J. (2008). *The 4 core factors for school success.* Larchmont, NY: Eye on Education. 51–54.

Williamson, R., & Blackburn, B. R. (2009). *The principalship from a to z.* Larchmont, NY: Eye On Education. 143–151.

Zepeda, S. J. (2007). *The principal as instructional leader: A handbook for supervisors.* Larchmont, NY: Eye On Education.